DRAMATISTS PLAY SERVICE, INC.
ERRATA SHEET

Insert for

AS BEES IN HONEY DROWN
BY DOUGLAS CARTER BEANE

Insert begins
on page 54

ALEXA. Look. I have to say the name, let me pick it.

MIKE. *(Points to the video and then watches her.)* Watch. And learn. *(Just like that she is Holly Golightly in* Breakfast at Tiffany's.*)*

ALEXA. Telephone is right there. No it's not, where did it get to? Oh, that's right. I put it in the suitcase so I wouldn't hear it when it rings. Where's cat. Poor cat. Poor slob. Poor no name slob. One day I'm going to find someplace where he and me can belong. I'm not sure where that is, but I know what it's like. It's like Tiffany's. I'm CRAZY for Tiffany's. *(Bossa nova music plays.)* Nothing too awful can happen to you there. I'm sorry you wanted something — oh right. Telephone. *(The rest of the room comes up along with the blue light. Mike hands her the telephone. She doesn't take it yet.)*

MIKE. Alexa Farquar.

ALEXA. A "v." A "v" to go with the "x."

MIKE. You know what? Lower the voice. *(Brenda looks at the set, the lights change, and she is suddenly Tallulah Bankhead in* Lifeboat.*)*

ALEXA. Did you see anything of Charcoal? Joe, the Porter. He helped me onto the lifeboat. What part of the ship were you on, darling? *(The scene is abruptly over. Mike shoves the telephone back at her.)*

MIKE. Alexa Vere de Vere.

ALEXA. Alexa Vere de Vere. *(They both laugh.)* We can't. No one in their right mind would believe a name like — *(An instant later.)* I can't.

MIKE. You can. Just talk.

AS BEES
IN HONEY
DROWN

BY DOUGLAS
CARTER BEANE

★

★

DRAMATISTS
PLAY SERVICE
INC.

For Mom

AS BEES IN HONEY DROWN was developed at the Drama Department. As far as I can tell, all 40 members did at least a reading of it and I can't thank them enough. It was also read at Portland Stage when Greg Leaming was at the helm with the following cast:

ALEXA	Kristin Nielson
EVAN	Bo Foxworth
PHOTOGRAPHER, et al	Jeff Hayenga
RONALD, et al	Kevin Geer
AMBER, et al	Kim Daykin
WAITER, et al	Lisa Benevides

and I can't thank them enough either. It was then workshopped at the late lamented Sundance Playwrights Festival when Jerry Patch was at the helm. (Is there a curse on this play for the Artistic Directors that choose it?) Anyway I thank them, but not enough.

The play's first production was by the Drama Department, where I am artistic director (hey, wait a minute). It opened June 19, 1997 at the Greenwich House. Directed by Mark Brokaw, sets by Alan Moyer, costumes by Jonathan Bixby, lights by Kenneth Posner, sound by David Van Tiegham. James FitzSimmons was the Stage Manager. The cast:

ALEXA	J. Smith Cameron
EVAN	Josh Hamilton
PHOTOGRAPHER, et al	Mark Nelson
RONALD, et al	T. Scott Cunningham
AMBER, et al	Cynthia Nixon
WAITER, et al	Sandra Daley

They all made me look good.

Four weeks later the play moved to the Lucille Lortel. Produced by Edgar Lansbury, Everett King, Randall L. Wreghitt, Chase Mishkin, Steven M. Levy, Leonard Soloway, by special arrangement with Lucille Lortel; and with Bo Foxworth going in for Evan, and Amy Ryan going in for Amber. New actors continue to go on and understudy, and I continue to look good. So they're doing their job.

I give my undying gratitude to Eric for inspiring the first act and Gene for inspiring the first act and Gene for inspiring the second.

Finally, this play wouldn't have happened if it weren't for Mark Brokaw, Mike Rosenberg, Mary Meagher, and Edgar Lansbury. And I know it.

CAST

This play is written to be performed with a cast of six. The actors play the following roles:

Evan Wyler
Alexa Vere de Vere
Photographer, Swen, Royalton Clerk, Kaden
Ronald, Skunk, Mike
Amber, Backup Singer, Secretary, Bethany, Ginny, a Second
    Muse
Waiter, Backup Singer, Carla, Newsstand Woman, Denise,
    Illya, a Muse

Part of the fun of the play is the four actors portraying all of glamorous New York. I wrote it that way and prefer that it be performed that way.

TIME

The present.

PLACE

New York City.

AS BEES IN HONEY DROWN

ACT ONE

"Life"

Scene 1

A photographer's studio.

A seamless. A light shines on Wyler, a handsome young writer. He is in his late twenties and he knows it. A flash of light as a Photographer scampers around with a camera. A beautiful photographer's assistant, Amber, stands next to a ladder sipping a glass of white wine.

PHOTOGRAPHER. Life. Life. A little more. I'm sorry, what is it you do again?
WYLER. I'm a writer.
PHOTOGRAPHER. That would explain it.
WYLER. What?
PHOTOGRAPHER. Why you're uncomfortable.
WYLER. That's the writer's job, isn't it? To be uncomfortable.
PHOTOGRAPHER. Amber, lose the shadow on his face.
AMBER. *(Adjusting a light.)* Amber wants to be dancing.
PHOTOGRAPHER. Quiet, Amber. So — what did you write?
WYLER. A novel. My first.
PHOTOGRAPHER. Amber, honey, more light.
AMBER. Amber wants to be dancing.

PHOTOGRAPHER. What's it about?

WYLER. Sorry?

PHOTOGRAPHER. Your novel, what's it about? Don't smile.

WYLER. It's this story of this guy who's in his twenties — *(He is suddenly plunged into darkness.)* Amber!!

AMBER. Amber says she's sorry. *(The light comes back on.)*

WYLER. — and this guy is like overwhelmed with this conflict of fantasy and reality —

PHOTOGRAPHER. Wyler, you any relation to —

WYLER. William Wyler, no. Nor Gretchen. My real last name is Wollenstein. And ... well that's a little long for a book cover. And — you know there really are no, you know, Jewish themes in my writing so —

PHOTOGRAPHER. And you kept your first name which is Evan and — *(He points at his camera, Amber looks in and focuses it for him.)*

WYLER. Actually my first name is Eric.

PHOTOGRAPHER. Oh.

WYLER. But I figured with the W and the Y in the last name, a V in the first name would look so good and —

PHOTOGRAPHER. Well, you kept your initials. You won't have to change your sheets.

WYLER. I hadn't really thought of —

PHOTOGRAPHER. Great. Let's lose the shirt.

WYLER. Sorry?

PHOTOGRAPHER. The shirt. Let's lose the shirt.

WYLER. Is there something else you want me to —

PHOTOGRAPHER. You look like you have a nice build.

WYLER. Oh. I see. You're thinking in terms of a shirtless thing.

PHOTOGRAPHER. Right. Amber, lose his shirt.

WYLER. You know — I just don't know if — And I'm probably way, way out on a limb here, but I was thinking more in the genre of like a pullover V neck and a button down shirt and, you know, kind of leaning on a stack of Proust and —

PHOTOGRAPHER. Filterless cigarette, long dangling ash?

8

WYLER. I don't smoke, but right.
PHOTOGRAPHER. No.
WYLER. No?
PHOTOGRAPHER. This is so endearing. Look. I don't want to put you down. I'm sure you have a very nice, trenchant, tortured, art-damaged life. In your exposed brick grubby railroad flat on West repel me street. Filled with filth and far too much Henry Miller and dank air clinging with clove cigarette smoke and nostalgia for Bennington. But, I'm here to sell magazines, you're here to sell books. So, lose the shirt. *(A moment. Amber is now at Wyler's side. He thinks for a moment. The Photographer goes over to set his camera in a different location. Wyler immediately removes his shirt.)*
WYLER. Selling books is selling books, right? *(He looks to Amber for encouragement.)*
AMBER. Amber wants to be dancing. *(Wyler hands his shirt to Amber. The lighting changes, a fan machine is now on. The feel is now sultry. The Photographer returns to the seamless.)*
PHOTOGRAPHER. Now take your right hand and grab your left shoulder. *(As Wyler does so.)* This isn't so bad, is it?
WYLER. No.
PHOTOGRAPHER. No. Not at all. Now … fuck the camera. *(A flash, then darkness.)*

Scene 2

The Hotel Paramount.

Resplendent in a simple black suit, Alexa toys with a strand of real pearls. A beautiful cape is draped over the back of her chair. A silver tea service and pastries are on the table. Wyler approaches the table. Alexa is now effortlessly sliding a cigarette into an ivory cigarette holder. She looks up, gently shaking her Louise Brooks bob.

ALEXA. Evan Wyler!

WYLER. Alexa Vere de Vere?

ALEXA. Lamb. I hardly recognize you from your photograph without your *mammilia*. Have some *petit dejuner,* though be warned the *dejuner* here is very *petite,* sit sit. *(Wyler does so.)* I have the most shimmering new screenplay for you to write. I pray that you'll forgive me for not going through your agent but the moment I read your book and I found that you were listed in the phone book, I —

WYLER. No, no that's OK.

ALEXA. I loved your book, did I say? I saw the semi-nude photo in a magazine and just lunged for a copy. It is fabulous and I NEVER use that word. You have got to do this movie!

WYLER. Thank you.

ALEXA. You are sans doubt my favorite new writer and, if Cheever is dead, you are my favorite living writer. The reason I called you is that I have been struggling — looking for *the* genius young writer to write this mouthwatering movie idea I have up my Gucci sleeve. David Bowie, no less, wants to play my father. He's a dear friend. David Bowie, not my father. Love this lobby, please. It's not so much a lobby as a lobby as told to Theodore Geisel. You see I want this film to be the story of my life which is too entrancing, almost even for me, I mean here I am in the blush of my youth and I am working with Morris Kaden of Delta records, do you know Morris Kaden of Delta records, how did you come to be such an amazing writer? *(She takes a sip of tea.)*

WYLER. Which tea are you drinking, the orange pekoe or the Sodium Pentothal?

ALEXA. Repartee! You are *brilliant.* God. I love writers. They always have the last word, because they know so many. Gore Vidal says that. I say it too. What do we ever get of any bygone civilization but the poems left behind. I'm part Indian, I know things. Do you think David Bowie is dark enough to pull off an Indian? I mean a red-dot Indian not a woo-woo Indian. Try the boysenberry, it's a revelation.

WYLER. Have you ever thought of diagramming these sen-

10

tences in your head before you speak them?

ALEXA. See, that's what I mean. Who else but a writer — they know so much about life, no one pulls the cashmere over the eyes of a writer. When I do my work in the music business I always say, "let me have lunch with the lyricist," you know that I'm a record producer, but you know that. Mostly in England, do you love England?

WYLER. I've never been.

ALEXA. You would love. Everyone is gay. Truly. When you say the queen, you have to specify. How they procreate is beyo — How long did it take you to write this debut novel, it is a debut novel please say, "yes."

WYLER. Uh … yes? Nine years.

ALEXA. And it's ever so thin.

WYLER. Well, I'm not — writing doesn't come easy to me. I'm not particularly good at listening to people and figuring out what's going on in their minds. Or summing up with a grand sweeping statement. But —

ALEXA. But?

WYLER. But I do know when to use a semicolon.

ALEXA. What you say is music to my ears, and I work in the music business, so — You're not a having any tea. Let's get down to cases. I am overt with joy about your book. There's a movie there, I just don't know that I'm in a position to make it right now.

WYLER. Right.

ALEXA. But I mean after our movie, who knows?

WYLER. Right.

ALEXA. What I'm doing right now is taking all my connections in record and film — I work in the recording industry, but you knew that — which are *legion* — and combining them to create a production company. I feel I've had enough success making money for other people to start making money for myself. You're a creative person, I'm sure you know the feeling.

WYLER. Yes, abso — yes.

ALEXA. My life has been nothing short of amazing. I mean I can't tell a total stranger three episodes and I must show you — *(She opens the contents of her purse on to the table.)* they are

11

emploring that I make a movie of it. I was married off by my mother when I was fourteen — I had to lie about my age, which is to be encouraged, but not a fourteen — to the son of a significantly rich person. Then my husband died. I was penniless. Cannot find it — don't overlook the butter — and that's where I changed my life, with my philosophy. *(She stops to take a pastry from the plate.)*

WYLER.   What's that?

ALEXA.   A brioche.

WYLER.   No, I mean your philosophy.

ALEXA.   *(She is now a hub of activity between her cigarette in a holder, her purse contents, her tea and her brioche.)* Well, I mean that's your job. As the writer. I only know that I'm living it. I need you to define it for me. Something to do with sketching out what you want to be and then coloring it in as it goes. Being what your dreams are, and … well, look at us now, I see your picture and just feel instinctively you know what I'm talking about. I read your book and now here we are at the Hotel Paramount over *petite dejuner* and great lashings of butter and I'm offering you one thousand dollars a week to write the story of my life and —

WYLER.   Really?

ALEXA.   Oh, God. Haven't I told you? I have absolutely no mind for money whatsoever, that's what accountants are for — *(From within her Judith Leiber jeweled egg, she pushes aside pills and make-up and pulls out a wad of cash.)* And agents, though I don't believe in agents, do you?

WYLER.   Mine is —

ALEXA.   Let's not deal with them. They are such unbearable leeches. Why should she get a hundred of your thousand? I introduced myself. Here we are one thousand dollars. *(She hands him a thousand dollars in twenties and a couple hundreds held together with a rubber band.)* I find that agents have no imagination. No taste for … possibilities.

WYLER.   Actually, I agree.

ALEXA.   Waiter! Let's keep this *entre nous*. I believe in cash, I think in this flighty world it's the only thing left with any impact. Now I don't see this taking more than a few months, the info gathering part and then we'll work out a juicy amount for you to actually write it. Remember David Bowie wants to play my father. Maybe Iman could play my mother? If he could be darkened and she could be lightened. *(A Waiter glides by.)* Check please. I mean does this interest you in any way, shape or form?

WYLER.   Does this interest me? In any way, shape or form? Well let's see. I've lived my life making sacrifices for the moment when I would see my first novel published. I've made sacrifices, lived sacrifices until this moment — I'm living in a place CNN would casually dismiss as third world. The people who are my age who don't do what I do have homes and cars and — I scrounge for subway fare. So I have my nine-years-in-the-making overnight success and you know? I'm thinking, oh this is where they pull back the velvet cord and I get to meet whomever I want to meet and do whatever I want to do and I'm still looking for fucking temp work to hustle together rent. Because no one ever tells you about that little breather period between critical success and financial success. Does this interest me in any way, shape or form? Yes. I would say this interests me in every way, shape and form.

ALEXA.   Happiness!

WYLER.   Just tell me what you need to know.

ALEXA.   Only one thing. I ask it before any business relationship.

WYLER.   What's that?

ALEXA.   If you absolutely had to sleep with one of the Three Stooges, which one would it be?

WYLER.   What? *(He starts to laugh.)*

ALEXA.   No really lamb, the answer reveals your personality. I mean if you say Moe, I know you wish to be dominated — *(Wyler laughs harder.)* Which I, of course, am incapable of, and if you say Larry, well, I mean, God help you.

WYLER.   I'm just trying to think of a situation where I would absolutely have to sleep with one of the three stooges.

ALEXA.   Too funny. Now darling, what shall I do? My accountant, Martel Grushkov, wants a record of all these businessy lunches, but won't let me have credit cards because I just see homeless people and I want to buy them socks. I'll need a receipt of some sort —

WYLER.   I could put this on my credit card and you can give me cash, if that could help.

ALEXA.   Such a help. *(Wyler puts his credit card down, the Waiter takes it away.)* I hate my accountant, I should have known something was up when he said, "Shemp." So, pick a stooge.

WYLER.   Curly.

ALEXA.   Oooh. Why on earth? Here's fifty dollars. *(She hands him two twenties and a ten.)*

WYLER.   That's too much.

ALEXA.   Please. So why Curly?

WYLER.   Because he would make that high pitched "Whoo whoo whoo" noise at the climax. *(The Waiter comes with the check and card, Wyler signs it. She shovels things back into her purse.)*

ALEXA.   The ONLY response. The Duke of Chichester, who would adore you, once told me, he's a brilliant international tax attorney, does all my claims, he told me Larry and when I said why he said so that he could hold on to the hair for dear life. *(Wyler laughs. She stands.)* This has been everything I hoped it would be and somehow just a little bit more. *(Wyler stands up and walks with her.)* We must start right away, I am feverish with enthusiasm. Now tomorrow is no good I've got — please let me hold your arm, there is no railing on this staircase and it unnerves me — *(She takes Wyler's arm and places her head on his shoulder. They walk down the staircase.)* I gave you money for the check, right?

WYLER.   Right.

ALEXA.   Curly and high pitched whoo whoo. Such genius. You were born for this life. Wyler. Are you Welsh?

WYLER.   Uh. Yeah.

ALEXA.   I could tell by your coloring. *A WELSHMAN.* I shall trust you anyway. Now. We shall begin. Tomorrow I must deal with rock stars and their egos. Not pretty, but Wednesday afternoon?

WYLER.   Sure.

ALEXA.   Just the afternoon, the night is fraught — your scent is tremendous.

14

WYLER. Ah — yeah — thanks —

ALEXA. But don't you adore the scent of soap on a man, you do love men don't you?

WYLER. Uh no. I don't love anyone. I sleep with men, but —

ALEXA. Oooooh. An emotional cripple, how enchanting! This way there can never be sexual tension between us, we can only be soul mates like Sally Bowles and Christopher Isherwood or Holly Golightly and whomever Truman Capote called himself. *(They are at the bottom of the staircase. They make their way to an elevator.)* Wednesday. Noon. Sixth floor of Saks. We've got to get you a suit before we lunch. Now if you will excuse me, I'm expecting a call from an investor in Milan who is, to put it mildly, endowed. *(She presses for an elevator, the door opens immediately to reveal a green lit elevator.)* Oh look, we *are* in Oz. So there. *(She steps in.)* I don't trust this elevator. Well, hold on to something tight, close your eyes and sing Shalom Alecheim. My late husband always used to say that, he was Jewish, I have no idea what he meant. *(The door begins to close.)* Hooray. Lots of love. *(The door is closed.)*

WYLER. Excellent.

Scene 3

The men's changing room, Saks.

Ronald, a very effeminate sales clerk, enters with a suit. Wyler is undressing.

RONALD. She's a goddess.

WYLER. She's kind of —

RONALD. A bright, green goddess.

WYLER. I mean, man, to live like that. Not having to worry about money. Signing for everything. And the people she knows and —

RONALD. You working with her?

WYLER. Ah, yes.

15

RONALD. I hate you. She only works with the flawless. Everybody she's ever found has done the sky rocket thing. She's got a real eye for it. What do you do?

WYLER. I'm a writer. I'm going to write the story of her life. As a screenplay. *(He is down to his underwear and socks.)*

RONALD. Wait a minute. I didn't think I could hate you more, and now I realize, I CAN!!! Here, try these on. 100% silk. Cry me a river. *(He hands Wyler a pair of socks. Wyler is changing his socks when the curtain is shucked aside and Alexa strides in, shirt in hand.)*

ALEXA. Lamb, this shirt —

RONALD. Boundaries, boundaries!

ALEXA. Oh now Ronald.

RONALD. Boys only in the changing room, no girls allowed. He-man woman haters club.

ALEXA. No fair, if I'm buying the suit I want to pick it out! I promise the milli-second a heterosexual male enters the room I shall scatter.

RONALD. Well — all right. But only because you're divine.

ALEXA. But gay men adore me, when in London I am FLANKED by the Pet Shop Boys! Lamb, the shirt, it's the ONLY solution for your frame. *(As Wyler puts on the shirt, Ronald and Alexa play.)*

RONALD. Have you seen the suit?

ALEXA. Happiness.

RONALD. If you see only one suit this season, let this be it!

ALEXA. Women will see Evan in this suit and die. Gay men will see Evan in this suit, squeal and die. Straight men will see Evan in this suit, be confused and die. Lesbians will inherit the earth.

RONALD. And I have a tie, a masterpiece of a tie, a Guernica of a tie to go with it! *(He is gone. By now, Wyler has his shirt on. Alexa hands him the slacks.)*

WYLER. Auntie Mame, long pants!

ALEXA. You behave or I'll tell Ronald you like him. Hurry Lamb, I crave to see you in this suit.

WYLER. Alexa, I don't really — I'm not entirely comfortable —

ALEXA. The shirt?

WYLER.   No. I just don't feel comfortable with you, after giving me a nice salary, just buying this suit for me. Please, let me pay for it.

ALEXA.   Lamb, my dearest lamb. You will buy other suits. You will buy hundreds, nay thousands of suits. You will buy suits in Italy, have them altered and shipped back to America. And they will sit in closets and you will never get to them and you will hand them down to assistants or housekeepers. This is the world that lies ahead for you. But this. This is your first suit. The suit you buy at the moment when you belong in a suit. It's a glorious moment. And you've let me share in it in some small way. And it is — and you are not allowed to laugh here, Lamb — it is thrilling. Please. You are letting me share in the honor of the moment. The payment of the suit. It is my admission. *(Wyler puts the slacks on. Alexa holds the jacket up for him in the subtle haberdasher manner. She has obviously done this before. He slides into it.)* There. There. You look ... you are ... sheer happiness.

WYLER.   *(Alexa leans forward and kisses him on the lips.)* What was that for?

ALEXA.   For luck! An old superstition I've just invented.

RONALD.   *(Sweeping in with a tie.)* Nicole Miller. I could kiss her on the lips with tongue.

ALEXA.   Shoes! What has been going on in my *petite tete? (She is running out.)* Evan, what size shoe do you wear?

WYLER.   Uh, twelve D. *(Ronald and Alexa exchange a look.)*

RONALD and ALEXA.   Hmmmmmmm.

WYLER.   Quit it. *(Alexa is gone with a laugh. Ronald ties the tie on Wyler.)* Have you — has Miss Vere de Vere tried suits on a lot of other people?

RONALD.   Here? A few. Also elsewhere around town. So I hear. And it's always the same. They come in and it's like you, I mean no offense, but who are you? Then a month later, they are the complete and total household name. And when they come back into the store they're big and famous and there's a fuss and ... they always see me and. Smile. Like we've shared a special moment or something.

WYLER.   I've never in my whole life, met anyone like her. I mean outside of a play or a book or a —

RONALD.   She's a mixture of every woman I've ever loved in a movie.

WYLER.   The way she is … so … amazing in every way. And yet just getting through a day seems a struggle for her. As strong and as powerful as she no doubt is, I want to protect her. Weird, huh?

RONALD.   Here's a little secret. Between you, me and the New York Post. If I were to fall in love with a woman, it would be her.

WYLER.   God. Same here. Maybe we're closet heterosexuals.

RONALD.   Impossible. Your suit hangs properly. Here. Look in the mirror. Get your bearings.

ALEXA.   *(Before Wyler can, Alexa's back! With an armload of shoes.)* Lamb, shoes in excelsia! I have cash for it all. Be a lamb and put this on your charge so my evil Shemp-loving accountant will have a record! Cologne! *(She's gone. Wyler looks into the mirror. He is mesmerized.)*

WYLER.   Wow.

RONALD.   Your first suit?

WYLER.   Yes. *(Ronald smiles knowingly and leaves. As soon as he is gone, Alexa reenters with a bundle of cash in her hands. Loose, an occasional hundred falling to the ground. She is also precariously balancing a tray of colognes and a suit bag.)*

ALEXA.   I have the cash and cologne. And I've picked out a cunning little Lagerfeld traveling suit for myself. It compliments your suit without matching it.

WYLER.   *(Taking the cologne tray.)* Alexa you're spilling money all over the —

ALEXA.   What care I? Calvin Klein fragrances! *(Ronald reenters picks up the fallen cash, hands it to Alexa, then hands the check to Wyler.)* Have you ever noticed that his scents capture a man in any contemporary relationship? First he wants you. *(She hands a bottle to Wyler who is signing a check. She then hands a hundred to Ronald.)* Obsession. Thank you, Ronald. Then he promises to build a life with you. *Eternity. (She hands a second bottle to the now fumbling Wyler.)* Then he realizes what he's in for. And he is out of there. *(She hands him a third bottle.)*

18

ALEXA, RONALD and WYLER. *ESCAPE!! (They laugh. Wyler is handed his receipt. Alexa takes back the bottle of* Escape *and is about to spray it on his neck. She hands the money to Wyler.)*
ALEXA. Here's the cash, *mon chou.* Ronald, what's our time?
RONALD. One o' —
ALEXA. THAT CAN'T BE THE RIGHT TIME!!! *(Wyler turns just then, getting a face full of sprayed* Escape. *Alexa takes the cash and shoves it into her pocket and gets up. She pulls the blinded Wyler along. Everything happens within a second.)* Lamb, we're late!
WYLER. Ow! *(They all laugh.)*
ALEXA. We're late for our meeting. *(She grabs Wyler by the arm and bolts. On the way out, Ronald hands them a large shopping bag.)*
RONALD. Here are Mr. Wyler's old clothes! *(Wyler and Alexa are gone.)* Come back soon.

Scene 4

Wyler's compostion book / Various.

First, Wyler holds a composition book. And a pencil.

WYLER. Notes on the life of Alexa Vere de Vere for eventual film script. Notes taken today. First in the limo. To the restaurant. *(He turns, he and Alexa are in the back seat of the limo.)*
ALEXA. And truly, India. Well, when the Montbattens — Montbatten — Boring, but hardly worth blowing up — left they took my mother, white, and father, red dot, with them to London, which explains my rollicking Kathleen Turner of an accent and — Oh look. You're writing in a faux marble composition book with a number two pencil. In an age of Powerbooks. *SMASHING.* Ah here we are! Now Lamb, this is the place. Let the Regency have its power breakfast, this is the power lunch. Fortunes come and go over appetizers. Once a Japanese business man started choking on a Caesar salad. Stock to half the American film companies went through the floor.

Everyone thought it was rage, but it was just a crouton. *(Back at the composition book.)*

WYLER.   Later, in the limo after lunch. *(Back in the limo. They are joined by a model, Swen.)*

ALEXA.   I remember when I first moved to London I was a child, you may want to write this down, and I turned to mother and I said, I don't care that father has squandered our inheritance on the tables with Princess Grace, I am not marrying that rich broker's son. But then I met Michael and let bygones be — *(Swen turns the radio on loudly.)* Swen, must you toy with the buttons?

WYLER.   I don't think he speaks English.

ALEXA.   I know but he is Nordic and he did a fashion layout that was nothing short of pornography and —

SWEN.   Yah, Yah. Photoshoot photoshoot.

WYLER.   Where are we going?

ALEXA.   The airport.

WYLER.   The airport?! I don't have —

ALEXA.   Relax, Lamb. We're not traveling anywhere, we're just picking up this *SIN*sational new band I'm signing, you'll adore. Swen? Rock and roll?.

SWEN.   Yah, yah! Rock and Rolla, Rock and Rolla!! *(Back at the composition book.)*

WYLER.   After the airport, in the limo. *(The limo now is packed with a rock singer, Skunk, his two Female Backup Singers and Swen. Alexa is talking to Wyler who is trying to get things down. The band is talking to Swen about music. A tape of a percussion track rattles the windows. Salted nuts and champagne are being passed around.)*

ALEXA.   My wedding was of course very simple, only five hundred, it was in so many tabloids and — it is far too noisy in here — *(Alexa pushes the button that opens the moon roof. She stands up and is outside. Wyler stands up and joins her.)* There, that's better. Such the cacophony. The wedding was part Jewish, owing to the groom and part, well, I asked my refreshingly unspiritual father what religion we were and he thought perhaps Hindu, and I couldn't have cows milling about so it just had this sort of Eastern feel. And — *(A bottle of champagne is handed up to them.)*

SKUNK. *(A cockney.)* Here ya go, Luv!

ALEXA. Bless you, Skunk. *(Back at the composition book.)*

WYLER. A restaurant who's popularity will last as long as any of the dairy items on its menu. *(Crammed around a table, Wyler, Alexa, Skunk, Swen and the two Backup Singers.)*

ALEXA. London was London then. The Clash, the Cure, the Smiths, the Pretenders, the Boy George, the parties, the pharmaceuticals, the beverages. I don't know what London is now. One day I awoke and it had become Luxembourg or something. How well I remember when my first release with Simon LeBon hit the airways. The critics were but peeling off cart — I stood there reading the reviews with my new discovery, Illya Mannon — well my mother could have written those reviews, not actually my mother, but my mother metaphorically. And I — dear ones, here I sit with my boys — I felt then no doubt how you two must feel. On the virtual circumference of fame. My Skunk. My Lamb. This meal has taken on a certain *Disney on Ice* quality. I feel I shan't recover.

BACKUP SINGER. Medallions of venison, anybody?

ALEXA. And here's Bambi! Now Skunk I have got the *only* state of the art recording studio set up for Thursday and —

SKUNK. Did that money exchange do the trick —

ALEXA. Utterly, and the accountant has a big bulging envelope for you, unmitigated bone head that I am I left it behind in his office, it is but winging it's way to your hotel. *(She opens her purse amidst all the food.)*

BACKUP SINGER. Oi! Luv!!

ALEXA. Let me give you something —

SWEN. Hey!

SKUNK. That's ok, that's ok. I'll get it later. We just got to make sure that there's a reverb at the — *(Alexa accidentally knocks over a drink. Mass confusion.)*

BACKUP SINGER. Oi! Oi!!

ANOTHER BACKUP SINGER. Bugger!!

ALEXA. I'm sorry is there Scotch in —

WYLER. Alexa!

ALEXA. — the veni — I didn't get the reverb!

SKUNK. Gotta have the —

ALEXA.   To much information in my brain. My circuits are overloaded.

SKUNK.   We gotta have a reverb!

ALEXA.   I'm having a breakdown!! There's too much going on!

WYLER.   Calm down, Alexa.

ALEXA.   I smell burning toast, someone take my pulse!!

WYLER.   Calm down, calm down. I'll take care of it.

ALEXA.   I'm so —

WYLER.   Just. Calm down.

ALEXA.   How could I have forgotten that which is so basic? I mean reverb.

WYLER.   I'll take care of it.

ALEXA.   I am pouting with intent. Look at my face.

WYLER.   *(Standing up.)* I'll take care of it. I'll call the studio, get a re- whatever for tomorrow —

SKUNK.   Verb.

WYLER.   Put it on my charge, we'll get Shemp to reimburse me. It is not the end of the world here. Relax.

ALEXA.   You are an angel. A cherub. I'm not entirely sure what a seraph is but you are that also. Here's the phone number for the studio. *(She hands him a slip of paper.)*

WYLER.   Got it.

ALEXA.   Oh, Lamb.

WYLER.   Don't worry.

ALEXA.   And on the back of that shard of paper is the number for Luis Vuitton. My new luggage set. Could you —

WYLER.   Credit card, big envelope. You would be so lost without me.

ALEXA.   Lifesaver.

SKUNK.   *(Teasing.)* Careful of him, he's a Welshman!

WYLER.   What?

SKUNK.   Can't trust him, he's a Welshman. Name like Wyler, and that dark hair, you can't fool me.

WYLER.   Oh. That. Yes. Welshman.

ALEXA.   *(Placing a hand on Wyler's cheek.)* My little Welshman. Oh. If I were a boy … the mischief we could manufacture. *(Back at the composition book.)*

22

WYLER.   The VIP lounge of an impossible-to-get-into-night-club. Pull back the velvet cord. *(The VIP lounge of a club. Music plays in the background. Alexa and Wyler sit and sip cocktails.)*

ALEXA.   And Michael, the Jewish husband of convenience turned to me and said, "we need time apart," and I said, "separate beds?," and he said, "separate cities," can you imagine my heartbreak? I was just — *(Enter a well-built woman, Carla, wearing barely anything.)* Carla!

CARLA.   Alexa, you used up old tart!! What brings you back to New York?

ALEXA.   Darling, I'm making the movie of my life, can you beat it? This is Evan Wyler, the writer, he's forming it for me, he wrote —

WYLER.   It's great to meet —

CARLA.   You wrote "Pig and Pepper." Love that. Alexa you didn't snatch up the film rights to that did —

WYLER.   No —

ALEXA.   No that's for someone far wiser than me.

CARLA.   He should have his agent call me.

ALEXA.   I'm acting as his agent now, his agent has but no imagination. We'll talk.

CARLA.   You look resplendent. Drinks, Friday?

ALEXA.   South of France, sorry. When I get back?

CARLA.   Deal. *(Carla and Alexa kiss-kiss as Carla exits.)*

ALEXA.   Proving that it is possible to be underdressed for this affair.

WYLER.   And that's how deals are made? No agents, no offices, no lawyers? Casually over cocktails.

ALEXA.   My love, that's how a culture is maintained. Lawyers and such are for later. Initially it's not even cocktails. It's people passing and selling films on their way to the rest room. Over lunch a film executive mentions an idea at his studio, suddenly three other studios have similar ideas in development. A record producer plays a new song on the Hampton Jitney, by Monday five other labels are trying to capture that sound. All of us, the creative people, tearing about trying to feed a nation's insatiable appetite for entertainment. Making truckloads of money we never see so that we can discover something

new and vivid to present to poor fun-starved modern civiliza-
tion. The new becoming old almost before we find newer new.
Humanity gasping for air under the weight of its own culture.
All holding on for dear life as we create fresher and fresher
possibilities. As bees in honey drown. This is it. This is what
you've wanted your whole life, isn't it? To be a part of it?
WYLER.   Yes. Of course. Who wouldn't?
ALEXA.   And so you are. With this movie. Our movie. Where
were we?
WYLER.   "Separate beds, separate cities."
ALEXA.   That may be our title. *(Back at the composition book.)*
WYLER.   And finally, at four in the morning, on the Staten
Island Ferry. Just because.

Scene 5

A Staten Island Ferry boat.

*Alexa stands at the railing. Wyler is by her side, holding the bag
of his old clothing.*

ALEXA.   Tell me how much these new earrings are worth it!!
God, look at that view! Try to include my new earrings in it.
WYLER.   Actually I was wondering if there was a way that —
ALEXA.   Lamb, I know what you're going to say. I've been so
self-absorbed of late and I —
WYLER.   No, that's not what I —
ALEXA.   Well, I have and I apologize. I just feel we're coming
up to the point where my philosophy begins and I don't want
to break the rhythm. As soon as I get past my husband's suicide
which is haunting —
WYLER.   It's not the — I'm just gathering all this information
and if I knew what I was working towards, I might —
ALEXA.   Oh, but a game plan. Of course. We'll talk a bit more
and then you can write a quick treatment — the perfect word,

as if films were somehow a cure! — just a twenty page description and then I'll go out and pitch it to the studios.

WYLER. But even as I'm writing, I —

ALEXA. We'll make a trip to Hollywood. Oh and look at your face light up. It truly is the finest word in the English language, far surpassing my other favorites — Complimentary and royalties.

WYLER. But I mean — oh God, this is going to come out so awkwardly. I shouldn't — I'm really bad at this and —

ALEXA. Lamb. Unknit that brow. And share.

WYLER. Alexa, this — everything I've been jotting down, about your past and your life it's all so —

ALEXA. What?

WYLER. Fictitious. I mean Mountbatten leaving India that would put you at least over fifty and you're — plainly not and —

ALEXA. I was born in India. I left India at an early age. All right, an occasional factoid has been enhanced. But — honey lamb. I know how to interest people. Don't let me go through this venture with a virtual arm tied behind my back.

WYLER. And your name ... is —

ALEXA. And how are Ma and Pa Wyler?

WYLER. That's not my — real name. That's —

ALEXA. You're not the person you were born. Who wonderful is? You're the person you were meant to be.

WYLER. What about the —

ALEXA. But enough of me. Even I grow tired. What of you?

WYLER. Me?

ALEXA. Yes, you. Mr. I-don't-love-but-I've-slept-with-men, what is your personal life?

WYLER. Huh? Oh. There's nothing to me.

ALEXA. Oh dear, you're not one of those I-am-a-camera types, I refuse to believe it.

WYLER. Sorry. No personal life. (*A pause as they look out at Manhattan.*)

ALEXA. Have you ever been in love?

WYLER. You start right at the top, don't you?

ALEXA. Yes?

WYLER.   Yes.

ALEXA.   Ahhhh.

WYLER.   Yes. Of course. Once. Where would creativity be without unrequited love, right? *(Alexa keeps looking off at the beautiful skyline.)*

ALEXA.   *(Quietly.)* Right right.

WYLER.   *(Into his drink.)* It's nothing, really.

ALEXA.   Tell me, if you dare.

WYLER.   Please. No big story. Honestly. Please.

ALEXA.   Please?

WYLER.   Nothing. No startling story never once before told. Just some guy. At school. Smart. And funny. And — what have you. From our like second time together he was there with the "I love you." Constantly. He would say it every time I did something correct or endearing. Just toss it out like a piece of liver to a finalist at the Westminster Dog show. And. And I couldn't say it back. Felt it but. Coward. After a couple of months together when I finally realized that perhaps this was what they'd been writing all those songs about and I was ready to, I don't know, speak my emotions? He turned to me, on a bright winter morning and told me that though he cared deeply for me, he was no longer — wait — interested in pursuing the physical side of our relationship. *(They look at one another. They both know.)* Charming. And then he left and I threw myself into writing and — it's not the newest story you'll ever hear.

ALEXA.   An acquaintance of mine, Bethany Vance, the alleged actress, at a party in London, I found out to be a masochist. No really. Whips, chains. Enjoyed to be tortured, as it were. I asked her what it was that inspired her to be treated poorly. She told me that the line between pain and pleasure was very thin indeed. I smiled to her ruefully and told her not to fret because the line between pain and love was virtually indistinguishable. *(Self-consciously, they both look at the skyline.)* But we're not like that, are we? We're not the ones people hurt. We are the creative people. We have art to protect us, even if our greatest creation gets to be ourselves. *(She takes Wyler's shopping bag and walks across the deck.)*

WYLER.   Hey!

26

ALEXA. Come!

WYLER. Where are you goi —

ALEXA. We are saying good-bye.

WYLER. To whom?

ALEXA. To the old you. And all his woes.

WYLER. And who will replace him?

ALEXA.   Lamb, I can't be expected to do everything. Say good-bye to the old you, Evan. First salute him. He has served you well. *(Wyler salutes the bag and laughs.)* And toast him that he may rest in peace. *(Wyler toasts the bag and takes a swig of his drink.)* Now say, "Good-bye."

WYLER. Good-bye, old me.

ALEXA. Good-bye, old you!! *(She hurls the shopping bag toward the mighty Hudson. Wyler watches it hit the water. He laughs. Softly, Alexa slides her hand along the rail and places it atop Wyler's. He looks into her eyes.)*

WYLER. You're confection. Pure confection. *(They look at one another again. They slowly kiss.)*

ALEXA. Lamb?

WYLER. Baaaaaaa. *(They kiss again.)*

ALEXA. Lamb. We should not be doing this.

WYLER. Under no circumstance.

ALEXA. I mean Boswell never became involved with Johnson.

WYLER. I would have heard about it.

ALEXA. Well, I mean, I never saw a photograph.

WYLER.   But then it was like seventeen twenty or something. *(They start to kiss again. Alexa suddenly stops.)*

ALEXA. You took your wallet and keys out of those old pants, right? *(They laugh and kiss more fervently.)*

Scene 6

A bedroom at the Hotel Royalton.

The lights slowly come up on Wyler, in slacks and shirt from his suit, writing in his composition book. Alexa enters in an oversized terry robe. She immediately plops on the bed and pulls her make-up and mirror out of a bag.

ALEXA.   Now Lamb —
WYLER.   Baaaaa.
ALEXA.   Please don't do that. I rather feel Shari Lewis' hand should be up your back. Don't look at me yet darling — haven't had a moment yet to dab on a foundation — How is our little film treatment — I think it's time we beat the path to Hollywoodland and shake those money trees.
WYLER.   You think? Already?
ALEXA.   This treatment will be — I'm wiring the Pulitzer committee, I swear to God, they are going to add a new category. Best American film treatment. *(They laugh.)* How is it coming along?
WYLER.   Well … slowly.
ALEXA.   Allow me to register my disappointment.
WYLER.   I'm not particularly good at listening to people and figuring out what is going on in their minds. Or summing up with a —
ALEXA and WYLER.   Grand sweeping statement.
ALEXA.   Yes. Semicolon. I recall. You're a very special sensitive person. And you deserve the finer things in life. A match. We are a match. Ying and yang or whatever. Hollywood? Do we dare?
WYLER.   Why not?
ALEXA.   Oh the possibilities. I've got us on the four o'clock. American. Two side by side. We have a meeting tomorrow at eleven AM. Hark unto us, Brothers Warner!
WYLER.   Great!
ALEXA.   Oh, the places we shall go!!
WYLER.   Excellent.
ALEXA.   Two o'clock, Paramount. Five o'clock, Fox. A bidding war by six, my humble estimation. Then, I'm off to the South of France, you come back to little old New York. We meet up again on Monday, and we decide where we shall go to write it. Something decadent I think. New Orleans. Jazz and louver

doors and the spirit of Tennessee Williams to bolster us on.

WYLER. Great.

ALEXA. Or an island. With no telephones.

WYLER. Hmmmmm.

ALEXA. Are you packed?

WYLER. For the island or New Orleans?

ALEXA. Los Angeles first, Lamb.

WYLER. Right, right. *(They laugh.)*

ALEXA. So you go home and pack, I'll pack. I'll meet you at one at JFK at the Admiral's club lounge. Oh and could you pick up a carton of Dunhills for me, I shan't have time, and an LA paper or something so we know what's the latest and —

WYLER. Alexa — *(He begins to turn around to see her.)*

ALEXA. Don't look, don't look. I'm a sight I'm sure. I haven't had time to dab on any make-up.

WYLER. We can't leave yet.

ALEXA. Why ever not?

WYLER. I haven't finished the treatment.

ALEXA. Oh that.

WYLER. I'm afraid there's something missing. In the story. It's a painful part. Maybe you don't want to deal with this first thing in the morni —

ALEXA. *(On the phone.)* Room service please. *(To Wyler.)* Why not? Fire away. This way the coffee and croissants will arrive just as I'm feeling my worse to cheer me. *(To room service.)* Coffee and croissants. *(She hangs up the phone and speaks to Wyler.)* There. Never venture down unless you have a ride back up. A skiing instructor once told me that, I've gone and found deeper meaning. Now, ask me anything, but don't look at me.

WYLER. Do you want to tell me about Michael? I mean, if you don't —

ALEXA. Dear God. Well. Michael. Mr. Michael Stabinsky. The name. He came to me at a time when I was — quite, quite low. I was what I imagine you would call a party girl. A London party girl. The type you see in the tabs still today clutching the arm of some ancient rock star with the byline "here with unidentified friend." The type whose love of fun and good

29

times only belies a deep, plangent self-loathing and — Maybe after coffee would be —

WYLER. If you'd rather.

ALEXA. No. No, we've started. Let's finish. Just promise you won't look at me. Michael. Well. He was not handsome in a traditional sense. But he found something in me that was — special. Perhaps the way I find something special in others. Maybe. Too Freudian a side stop, I'll continue. And he became — smitten, obsessed with me. He was very much not of this century. Old world, if you will. I had seen him at countless, endless parties but never knew his — his father called upon my father. And set up an agreement for marriage. Surreal, no? The financial rewards for Father were ... tangible. He and my mother forced me to marry him. I did not love him. Then. He was hardly attractive in a, as I say, traditional meaning of the word. But we married and — the comfort which that afforded was what I imagined. But what I didn't count on, what I didn't bank on was — the world he would show me. A way of life. A way of possibilities. The casual way with which he, because he was so bloody rich, could breeze through life and meetings and get things done. And he loved me so. So ceaselessly. And I came to love him. And after we were married a year and had taken those pointless religious and legal vows, we took new vows. Profound vows. Vows of true love. For eternity. He nurtured me, again as I do others now, he "Found my genius" as he loved to say. He set me up in business. My connections in rock music from the party days were ... extensive. I became a manager. He was so ungodly proud. But that life, any life in the entertainment field — Phone calls, meetings, triumphs, disasters. Barely keeping afloat in the sticky sweet success. As bees in honey drown. Soon ʼe became abandoned. All my good fortune. And he felt resentful of my success. He was sick of people asking at parties what ʼ was that he ... did. And one morning, in the middle of several overwhelming negotiations he called me, sobbing, to say that he ... felt no longer a part of my life. And I, on a car phone whisking on to God only cares what now, Filofax on my lap. Cellular ringing at my side. Glibly snapped, "then do something about it." *(She begins to cry. Wyler begins to turn.)* Please don't look

30

at me. And when I returned late that night to my Chelsea flat. All was as it always had been. The candles blazing for dinner. The Mahler playing. And when I walked into the bathroom. Please don't look at me. He knew, you see that after a tense day at work I needed, nay REQUIRED, to unwind in a hot bath. "Why not give up this life, if you need to unwind from it?" He always said. Always. And.... When I walked into that bathroom the SHOCK, the near electric shock. First of tile smeared with red red blood. Then in the bathtub. The tub, he knew that I would be heading for. His lifeless body. The wrists gashed with shaving razors. Blood and life escaping and —

WYLER. Oh God.

ALEXA. Don't look at me. An arm extended from the bathtub on to the floor and a steady stream of — Don't look at me. *(Wyler looks at her.)* Don't look at me. *(She turns away.)* Don't. Look. I am not what I appear to be. I am nothing. I am a worthless half-caste piece of shit from the London streets. Who has truly only ever been loved by one man. An ugly, unattractive, generous man who gave me my life and I destroyed him. Don't look at me. *(Wyler moves to the bed.)* Please don't. *(He gently takes her chin in his hand and moves it towards him.)* I'm nothing, don't look at me.

WYLER. I —

ALEXA. I am nothing.

WYLER. I —

ALEXA. I am not to be loved by anyone.

WYLER. I — I love you.

ALEXA. No one should love me.

WYLER. Evan Wyler loves you.

ALEXA. Don't look —

WYLER. I'm looking at you. And I still love you.

ALEXA. Don't. Ever leave me. Don't ever leave me. Ever.

WYLER. I love you.

ALEXA. And I ... I love you. *(They kiss passionately.)* I love you, lamb. *(They begin to make love as the lights fade.)*

Scene 7

A newsstand.

A little shop. Covered with magazines all with smiling pretty people. Wyler walks in. A Woman attendant is there. Wyler looks at all the smiling pictures. He turns to the woman.

WYLER.   A carton of Dunhill cigarettes. And — do you have any Los Angeles papers or magazines that say what's going on there? I'm going to LA and I need to know what's —
WOMAN.   Just a moment, I'll check. *(She goes. Wyler picks up a copy of a magazine and quickly riffles through to find his picture. He does and smiles. Just then Skunk walks in. Wyler sees him first.)*
WYLER.   Skunk, my pictures in this magazine, did you see?
SKUNK.   *(He is furious.)* You!!
WYLER.   Hey, what's —
SKUNK.   You tosser, where the fuck is me money? *(He punches Wyler.)*
WYLER.   What the —
SKUNK.   You toerags owe me soddin' three thousand quid I put up. You and —
WYLER.   What are you — *(Skunk punches him again. Wyler is now bleeding.)* STOP!!
SKUNK.   You and that bloody slag Vere de Vere. You soddin' having me on? You having me on?
WYLER.   I didn't take any — *(Skunk punches him again.)* I didn't take any of your bloody money, look. *(Skunk threatens to punch him again.)* STOP!! Calm down. There's a mistake, an obvious mistake. I haven't taken anybody's money.
SKUNK.   That cunt Alexa did and you bugger well work with her and —
WYLER.   I don't work — I'm just writing with her and —
SKUNK.   Flight from London, studio space, hotel all on me bloody tab and she never gave me nothing —
WYLER.   I don't know anything about —

SKUNK.   I can't even fucking get a hold of her or find her and —

WYLER.   She has a meeting with you right now with Morris Kaden of —

SKUNK.   Who the bollocks is that? *(The Woman enters.)*

WOMAN.   Hey hey! Take this outside.

WYLER.   I swear I don't —

SKUNK.   Bullshit, you know.

WOMAN.   I'm calling the cops!

SKUNK.   You're a fucking grifter like her —

WOMAN.   *(Into the phone.)* Yes, there's a fight going on here at —

WYLER.   I don't know — I don't know!

SKUNK.   Tosser! Who are you anyway?

WYLER.   Wyler. Evan Wyler.

SKUNK.   How do I know that? You're bugger well Alexa's assistant — *(He punches Wyler again. Wyler's face is covered in blood. The Woman screams.)*

WYLER.   I am me.

SKUNK.   Who the fuck are you? *(A final punch from Skunk. And a shove. Wyler lands on the newsstand. The hundreds of smiling faces cover his face.)*

Scene 8

A pay phone.

Morris Kaden's office.

The Royalton.

Wyler is now covered in blood. his face is cut. He holds a hand-kerchief up to his left eye. He is at a street pay phone. He dials information.

WYLER.   It's a business. Delta records. *(A pause as he gets the number. He hangs up, puts a quarter in and dials.)* Yes. Morris

Kaden please. (*A pause as the lights come up on the outer executive offices of Delta records, a stylish Secretary is on a headset, lazily flipping through a magazine.*) Morris Kaden please.

SECRETARY. And who may I say is calling?

WYLER. Just put me through to Morris Kaden.

SECRETARY. I'm sorry Mr. Kaden doesn't speak to anyone unsolicited. And he does not return phone calls.

WYLER. Tell him this is about Alexa Vere de Vere, his employee.

SECRETARY. I'm sorry, that name again?

WYLER. Alexa Vere de Vere.

SECRETARY. I'm not familiar with that name at all.

WYLER. You probably haven't heard of her.

SECRETARY. Hon, trust me. I've heard of everyone.

WYLER. I'll hold.

SECRETARY. I'll hang up. (*She hangs up, the lights go out on her. A dial tone.*)

WYLER. Shit! (*He slams the phone against the receiver. Quickly dials another number.*) In Manhattan. Royalton Hotel. (*He gets the number. Puts in a quarter and quickly dials. The lights come up on the Clerk at the Royalton.*)

CLERK. Royalton.

WYLER. Alexa Vere de Vere. Suit 719.

CLERK. One moment. (*A moment.*) Ms. Vere de Vere has left for the South of France.

WYLER. Oh God.

CLERK. Is this Mr. Wyler?

WYLER. (*Hopefully.*) Yes, Evan Wyler. Has she left a note?

CLERK. Mr. Wyler. We have an outstanding bill here of three thousand dollars. Ms. Vere de Vere said you'd take care of it. (*The lights come up on a too trendy bar. Denise, an up-and-coming actress, enters. Alexa stands up.*) We've called on your credit cards and it appears you've reached your limit.

DENISE. Alexa Vere de Vere?

WYLER. Oh God.

CLERK. Mr. Wyler?

ALEXA. Cabbage!

CLERK. Is there another form of payment possible?

34

ALEXA.   I saw the magazine photograph of you in that dingy little play and I knew then and there that you must star in the movie of *MY LIFE!*

WYLER.   Oh my God. Hasn't she left a note? *(He slowly sinks to the ground and sobs.)*

CLERK.   No. She's gone to Toulouse to think. She said you would take care of the bill.

ALEXA.   We will away to Hollywood where we shall incite them to madness!

WYLER.   *(Through sobs.)* It isn't true.

CLERK.   Mr. Wyler? Mr. Wyler? Mr. Wyler, I can hear that you're still there, Mr. Wyler? Mr. Wyler?

WYLER.   It isn't true. It isn't true, isn't true!

END OF ACT ONE

ACT TWO

"Art"

Scene 1

A glamorous dinery, to be sure.

Another trendy restaurant. Alexa is talking with Denise.

ALEXA.   Art. Art. Art art art. *Je suis* knocked out by art. The homes of Hollywood are all about art, I cannot wait to show you. All modern and post modern works have found themselves in Los Angeles County. San Andreas goes? The last six pages of Janson's, gone. Ross Bleckner is in every living room in Bel Air. And some of his paintings. Of course you ask any of these movie people why they have this art in their life and never ever in their work and oh the blank stares. In their minds it is all a sort of aesthetic penance. You shall see when we're there!

Scene 2

Morris Kaden's office/various.

Morris Kaden is going over some papers with his Secretary. Wyler stumbles in. The Secretary sees him first.

SECRETARY.   Oh Christ, I'm calling security. *(She runs to a phone.)*
WYLER.   What the fuck is going on?
KADEN.   Who is this putz? Do I know this putz? Putz, who are you?

36

SECRETARY. *(At the phone now.)* We do not know this putz. I'm calling security.

WYLER. Something fucked up is going on with one of your producers.

SECRETARY. This putz is unknown to us.

KADEN. Which producer?

WYLER. Alexa Vere de Vere.

SECRETARY. She doesn't work here.

KADEN. She doesn't work here.

SECRETARY. We've never even heard of her.

KADEN. I've heard of her.

SECRETARY. You have?

KADEN. You — putz — what's his name?

SECRETARY. I don't know.

WYLER. Wyler. Evan Wyler.

KADEN. Wyler Evan Wyler, sit down. *(To his Secretary.)* Don't call security. Get this putz some damp paper towels and some Band-Aids. Hold all calls.

SECRETARY. *(As she exits.)* I don't know this putz, I don't know this producer and I know everyone.

KADEN. *(Offers Wyler a glass of water.)* Here putz. Water. Drink. So. Alexa Vere de Vere, huh? God. Haven't heard that name for a while. How much did she take you for?

WYLER. Take? What do you — I don't get it.

KADEN. She took you. Which word eludes you? She, the subject. Took, the verb, vernacular for took advantage of. You. The direct object. *(The secretary reenters. Hands the paper towels and bandages to Wyler.)*

WYLER. Oh no. Oh God.

KADEN. And from the looks this is very direct. Wyler Evan Wyler, God. Why don't you hand your credit card to my secretary so that she can see how much has been run up? *(Wyler does so.)*

WYLER. I think there's been a mistake. *(As the Secretary exits, he stands up.)*

KADEN. *(To his Secretary.)* Come in as soon as you know the amount. *(She is gone, he turns to Wyler.)* If you don't sit down now, I'm either going to laugh at you or cry for you. *(Wyler sits.)* OK.

Alexa Vere de Vere. Let's start at the beginning. What magazine were you in?

WYLER.   Magazine, how did you know — why?

KADEN.   And was the unbearable adjective "Hot" used at anytime and not in reference to temperature?

WYLER.   Hot writer.

KADEN.   How literary. That is how you were you found. Alexa, she — *(Lights come up on a stack of trendy magazines. Alexa is rifling through a magazine.)* pours through those magazines as if, well, as if they really mean anything, until she finds someone who is in some editor's estimation — *(Alexa rips out the page with Wyler's picture in it.)* Hot. *(The lights go out on Alexa.)* She contacts them with some harebrained scheme about working together. Some album, or television show, or Broadway musical or whatever that particular artist would consider doing to get some quick vast cash. Take the money and run type of scenario. Some — *(He stops to think of a word. The lights come up on Alexa. She is at the Hotel Paramount. We are back at their first meeting.)*

ALEXA.   … this most mouthwatering —

KADEN and ALEXA.   Movie idea —

ALEXA.   I have up my Gucci sleeve.

KADEN.   Whatever. Just enough to blow some sunshine up your ass. And the names get dropped.

ALEXA.   David Bowie, Iman, Morris Kaden, the Duke of Chichester etc. etc. etc.

KADEN.   And the places.

ALEXA.   London, India, Hollywood, South of France, an investor in Milan, Oz.

KADEN.   And the disregard for money and prices and — basically the world everybody wants to live in. *(The Secretary reenters.)* Oh and the support team.

ALEXA.   My lawyer, my international tax attorney, My Shemploving accountant. And agents, though I don't believe in agents, do you?

SECRETARY.   Mr. Kaden.

KADEN.   Yes?

SECRETARY.   Just shy of fifteen grand.

WYLER.   Oh my God.

KADEN.   You got off easily.

SECRETARY.   *(Handing the card back to Wyler.)* They said I should destroy the card in front of you with scissors. You look like you've already been through enough today. *(She exits.)*

KADEN.   That's how she lives. Almost famous person to almost famous person. She knows you're champing at the bit to lose the almost and just be famous. See, first you're blinded by the appearance and the jewelry, then it's the cash. The cold green cash. The bait.

ALEXA.   I read your book and now here I am at the Hotel Paramount over *petite dejuner* and great lashings of butter and I'm offering you one thousand dollars a week to write the story of my life and —

WYLER.   *(In a trance in Kaden's office.)* Really?

ALEXA.   Oh God. Haven't I told you? I have absolutely no mind for money whatsoever.

KADEN.   And she puts a thousand dollars in cash into your hand. With — wait, what does she say —

KADEN and ALEXA.   I believe in cash, I think in this flighty world, it's the only thing left with any impact. *(Alexa holds up the cash.)*

KADEN.   A nice appearance. A little glamour, cash in your hand. Let the games begin. And they do. With the first bill, she sets a precedent.

ALEXA.   Now darling, what shall I do? My accountant wants a record of all these businessy lunches, but won't let me have credit cards because I just see homeless people and I want to buy them socks.

KADEN.   And she's so helpless.

ALEXA.   I'll need a receipt of some kind.

KADEN.   And you're helpful.

WYLER.   I could put this on my credit card and you can give me cash.

KADEN.   So helpful.

WYLER.   If that could help. *(A Waiter breezes in and takes Wyler's credit card.)*

ALEXA.   Such a help.

KADEN.   And of course she pays you back immediately. The

39

first time.

ALEXA. *(Showing two twenties and a ten.)* Here's fifty dollars.

KADEN. With too much.

WYLER. That's too much.

ALEXA. Please.

KADEN. But also another precedent is set. One of distraction during the transaction. *(The Waiter is back with a check for Wyler.)*

ALEXA. *(As he signs it.)* If you absolutely had to sleep with one of the Three Stooges, which one would it be? *(The Waiter takes the check.)*

KADEN. Those distractions are important.

ALEXA. *(Now standing next to Wyler.)* What care I? Calvin Klein fragrances. Have you noticed that his scents capture a man in any contemporary relationship?

KADEN. Because soon comes the first one where money doesn't exchange hands.

ALEXA. *(She hands money to Wyler. Wyler reaches for it.)* This can't be the right time! *(She sprays cologne in his face.)* Escape! *(Wyler sees that the money has not been handed to him as she runs off.)*

KADEN. And soon you never see cash again. It's all on your credit card. Can't call the police on her. You've been volunteering to pay. *(A light on Alexa admiring a beautiful diamond bracelet.)*

ALEXA. And I've picked out this cunning little Lagerfeld traveling suit for myself. It compliments your suit without matching it. And on the back of that shard of paper is the number for Louis Vuitton. My new luggage set. And tell me how much these earrings are worth it!! *(Wyler covers his ears.)* And I simply must pick up the oh so many things I phone ordered while you were writing. *(Lights down on Alexa.)*

KADEN. You've helped pay for Alexa's five star, world class life. She gets the hot person to pay for her life and she is gone by the time the credit card bill arrives. On to the next hot person. She knows, her one bit of brilliance is that she knows. At that moment in time, when the artist first stands at the what — *(Lights up on Alexa in the nightclub.)*

ALEXA. All of us creative people —

KADEN. Brink of success, they call it.

ALEXA. Tearing about trying —

KADEN. The artist wants to be —

ALEXA. — to feed a nation's insatiable appetite for entertainment.

KADEN. Through the looking glass.

ALEXA. Making truckloads of money we never see —

KADEN. Ready to abandon all morals and logic.

ALEXA. So that we can discover something new and vivid —

KADEN. Ready to be famous and, so it would follow, fulfilled.

ALEXA. — to present to poor fun-starved modern civilization.

KADEN. Ready to lose all problems.

ALEXA. The new becoming old almost before we find the newer new.

KADEN. Ready to lose the old life.

ALEXA. Humanity gasping for air under the weight of its own culture.

KADEN. You're ready to sign anything.

ALEXA. All holding on for dear life as we create fresher and fresher possibilities.

KADEN. Anything not to have to be you, anymore.

ALEXA. As bees in honey drown. *(She disappears.)*

WYLER. How many has she done this to?

KADEN. A lot. Hundreds maybe. A lot of new people all the time in magazines.

WYLER. Why don't they stop her?

KADEN. Well — it's a pretty elite club, the survivors of Alexa Vere de Vere. Nice company to be in. And who really wants to go public and brand themselves as a stooge? Or worse, someone who pursues fame? And well, maybe there's a bit of gratitude for the dear girl. Nothing like the first big screw. The screw that toughens the skin for all the future screw attempts. You know, Teacher says every time an artist is screwed, an angel gets his wings.

WYLER. Doesn't anyone ever get her back?

KADEN. Most people have lives. They move on.

WYLER. I'm not — I don't think I'm going to move on. I'm going to get her back. And I'll get my money back.

KADEN. Wyler Evan Wyler. She doesn't have it to give back.

41

Move on. Why bother?

WYLER. Fifteen grand?!

KADEN. Consider it tuition.

WYLER. I'm different than — We slept together.

KADEN. Not unheard of with her. Just let go.

WYLER. You don't understand. I slept with her. And I'm gay.

KADEN. What do you want frequent flyer miles? Forget about it.

WYLER. She said she loved me. I told her that I loved her. I'm not big on — I hadn't done that before. *(A look of great sadness passes Kaden's face. He leans over and feels the material on the lapel of Wyler's suit.)*

KADEN. Well ... it is a great suit. If nothing else she made you buy yourself a nice suit. Her taste in suits —

WYLER. So — Oh God. So then — ?

KADEN. Even I was a putz once. Why do you think I'm the expert? *(Wyler stands up to leave.)* Don't. Please. Just leave her be. *(Wyler is at the door.)* We all let her go on because in an odd way, she reminds us what we were foolish enough to think of giving up. To have her life. Her sad empty life. We all actually considered giving up ourselves.

WYLER. What do you know about her that's true?

KADEN. Oh. None of her. One hopes.

WYLER. You know where I might talk to someone who might know something about her?

KADEN. Geez. Uh. Off hand, not really. Maybe. You know who might know about her is the dancer, what's her name Illya —

Scene 3

The telephone.

Wyler's composition book.

Immediately following the last scene, Wyler has his composition book. He leafs through and finds a mention in his notes.

42

WYLER.   Illya —

KADEN.   Illya Mannon. *(We see Alexa. She is as Wyler has written her on the page.)*

ALEXA.   I stood there reading reviews with my new discovery Illya Mannon. *(Illya Mannon appears. She is on the phone.)*

WYLER.   *(Now on the phone with Illya.)* Illya Mannon?

ILLYA.   Speaking.

ALEXA.   I stood there —

KADEN.   And there was that boy dancer in that video.

WYLER.   I'd like to talk to you about Alexa Vere de Vere.

ALEXA.   Quaking.

KADEN.   Going to be big.

ILLYA.   Oh Jesus. She still alive?

WYLER.   What do you know about her that's true?

KADEN.   And the sculpture performance person.

ILLYA.   Who is this? You get taken by —

WYLER.   Yeah.

ILLYA.   Yeah well. Join the crowd.

KADEN.   And that composer. With the animation.

WYLER.   I want to find her. And I'm looking for — for want of a better word, the truth. Something to help try to find her.

ILLYA.   What are you going to do once you find the truth?

WYLER.   I haven't thought that far in advance.

ILLYA.   Uhm. Well. You know I really don't know her. It was like one weekend and twenty-five grand. But you know who would know is —

KADEN.   And the actress with the accents.

ALEXA.   An acquaintance of mine — *(Evan leafs through the composition book.)*

ILLYA, KADEN and ALEXA.   Bethany Vance —

ILLYA.   She spent some real time with her —

ALEXA.   The alleged actress.

ILLYA.   She really got taken.

ALEXA.   At a party in London.

WYLER.   Bethany Vance? *(Bethany appears. She is on the phone.)*

ALEXA.   I found out to be —

BETHANY.   Yes?

ALEXA.   A masochist.

43

BETHANY. She said I was a masochist?

ALEXA. No really. Whips, chains.

BETHANY. You know that is just so typical, fucking typical. Fucker rips you off and then claims you into a circle of friends and then pins like intimate knowledge on you. But then, you know, I found out that like all her quote friends are people she's conned. All of them. The accountant, Martel Grushkov.

ILLYA. The investor from Milan.

KADEN. The Duke of Chichester.

ALEXA. Morris Kaden.

WYLER. Morris Kaden —

BETHANY. Morris Kaden, they're all alive and well and she's conned them. *(Wyler is now flipping through the pages of his book.)*

WYLER. The truth.

ALEXA. Illya Mannon, Bethany Vance, The Duke of Chichester,

ILLYA. That actor with the really great hair who can't act.

WYLER. I'd like the truth.

BETHANY. That singer with the six note range.

WYLER. Just someone tell me the truth.

KADEN. That poet who can't rhyme.

WYLER. Overseas operator, London. I'm looking for a residence for the Duke of Chichester.

ALEXA. Martel Grushkov, my husband deserted me in the most farfetched ways.

WYLER. Chichester, I guess.

ALEXA. The Pet Shop Boys.

BETHANY. And you know. What's his name? Him.

ILLYA. And Morris Kaden.

KADEN. Any putz.

BETHANY. The really famous one.

ILLYA. Did I mention Morris Kaden?

BETHANY. The celebrity.

ALEXA. The Clash, the Cure — My late husband always used to say that, he was Jewish.

WYLER. So you would agree that the names she drops are mostly people that she's conned?

ALEXA. The Boy George, Simon Le Bond, I am not marrying that rich broker's son, but then I met Michael.

WYLER. What about the husband who died?

ALEXA. Dear God.

WYLER. Michael.

ALEXA. Well Michael.

BETHANY. Who's Michael?

ALEXA. Mr. Michael Stabinski.

ILLYA. He's dead?

ALEXA. That name.

KADEN. Who's dead?

ILLYA. I thought he tried to kill her and she ran away.

BETHANY. I don't know a Michael.

ILLYA. Or he ran away.

BETHANY. Now a *MICHELLE* —

ILLYA. Somebody ran away. To Denmark.

KADEN. Is this the fiancée who died in the freak hovercraft accident?

WYLER. I think he's dead.

BETHANY. Why?

WYLER. Alexa told me.

KADEN. PUTZ!

ALEXA. His lifeless body. The wrists gashed with shaving razors and —

WYLER. You think he's still living?

BETHANY. If he exists at all.

ALEXA. The wedding was part Jewish owing to the groom and —

WYLER. He's in England maybe.

KADEN. Says her. Try New York.

ILLYA. I never bought that Indian princess crap.

BETHANY. Indian? Indonesian.

KADEN. Or Iranian.

BETHANY. Ah, she's probably American and so's her probably living dead husband. Or girlfriend.

KADEN. Try New York, then try London.

ILLYA. And then Denmark. Maybe. *(All, save Alexa and Wyler leave the stage.)*

ALEXA.   Dear God. Well Michael.

WYLER.   *(He is now on the phone with Mike.)* Michael Stabinsky?

ALEXA.   Mr. Michael Stabinsky. *(Mike appears.)* That name.

MIKE.   Mike.

ALEXA.   And Michael, the Jewish husband of convenience —

WYLER.   But Stabinsky?

MIKE.   Right, what can I do for you?

WYLER.   Are you the Michael Stabinsky — I'm sorry I'm just trying to track somebody down and you're in New York and this person is probably in London but — God. By any chance, are you the Michael Stabinski that knew — or do you know — Alexa Vere de Vere?

MIKE.   Yeah, sure.

ALEXA.   An ugly unattractive generous man who gave me my life and I destroyed him. *(Alexa disappears.)*

MIKE.   Wait. Oh God. You get taken?

WYLER.   Yeah. I can't believe that —

MIKE.   Oh. I'm sorry. And how did I die this time?

WYLER.   Oh my — Are you — In a bathtub. Suicide.

MIKE.   Bathtub. *(A moment as he thinks.) Death of Jean Paul Marat* by David. Right. She tends to kill me off as great works of art. I've gone down on ship, *Raft of the Medusa*, died in her arms, the *Pieta*. I think it's only a matter of time before I get struck by arrows like St. Sebastian. Listen, I'm sorry. I don't know anything about her whereabouts. I have absolutely no contact with her — haven't for years.

WYLER.   Could I —

MIKE.   Sorry?

WYLER.   Could we … talk about her.

MIKE.   Why would you want to do that?

WYLER.   I just would like to know the truth.

Scene 4

Mike's loft.

The Eighties.

First, the loft. Wyler sips a cup of coffee handed to him by Mike. A shutter runs up his spine and then he smiles.

WYLER. Hmmm.
MIKE. Good?
WYLER. Sure. Coffee?
MIKE. Bless you for noticing.
WYLER. No, it's good, it's — *(Mike takes a sip from his own cup and immediately spits it back into the mug.)*
MIKE. It's tar. Sorry, it's been on all day.
WYLER. It's OK.
MIKE. No, it's not.
WYLER. You're right, it's not.
MIKE. Then why did you say it was?
WYLER. I was being charming.
MIKE. Oh. Well. I don't do charm.
WYLER. Got it.
MIKE. I'll put new coffee on.
WYLER. So, tell me how you met Alexa.
MIKE. What did she tell you about me?
WYLER. Oh. Uh — *(He looks in his composition book.)* That you were older. Than — well her.
MIKE. I am. So far, so good.
WYLER. Old money. European.
MIKE. Sorry, no. Pennsylvania. Po' white trash.
WYLER. Jewish.
MIKE. Close. Catholic.
WYLER. Unattractive.
MIKE. Your call.
WYLER. No, you're cute.
MIKE. Really, how cute?
WYLER. Don't … milk it, you're cute.

47

MIKE.   Fair enough. Anything else?

WYLER.   Uh…. You were married. To each other.

MIKE.   No.

WYLER.   Lovers?

MIKE.   Not likely. I'm queer.

WYLER.   Yeah well, that's not exactly a brick wall ending for her.

MIKE.   So —

WYLER.   More just a speed bump.

MIKE.   You're queer?

WYLER.   Yeah.

MIKE.   Oh. So. And you think I'm cute?

WYLER.   Let's not — I'm not pursuing that right — You really don't do charming. You're direct.

MIKE.   That's 'cause I tell the truth. Only people who are deceitful have to be charming.

WYLER.   Well maybe a little charm —

MIKE.   Probably right. I'm over compensating for lessons learned young. What else did she tell you about me?

WYLER.   Uhm … *(He looks in the book again.)* —impossible Polish last name which is —

WYLER and MIKE.   Stabinsky.

MIKE.   True.

WYLER.   And that you discovered her and created her which is probably —

MIKE.   True.

WYLER.   False. True? Really?

MIKE.   Yeah.

WYLER.   But you — I thought you just said — about not being charming but truthful and —

MIKE.   Overcompensating for lessons learned young.

WYLER.   Got it. So — what do you mean, you created her?

MIKE.   Why do you want to know?

WYLER.   I'd like to know what makes a person this way —

MIKE.   And you want revenge?

WYLER.   Maybe. Or get my money back. Make sure she doesn't do it again.

MIKE.   Revenge strikes me as such the colossal waste of time. Look. What do you do?

WYLER.   I'm a writer.

MIKE.   Why don't you just go off and write something. Forget about Alexa.

WYLER.   I can't write.

MIKE.   *(Sarcastically as he gets the coffee.)* Yeah yeah, you can't write.

WYLER.   I mean I can't write.

MIKE.   Are you serious? *(He is taken aback.)*

WYLER.   It isn't just the money that Alexa stole from me. She stole my arrogance. The arrogance it takes to just shamelessly write something and assume someone, anyone might read it. The gall to think I might be a success. It's gone. Killed. I can't. I'm blocked. I can not write.

MIKE.   Oh God. I had no idea. I'm so sorry. I —

WYLER.   Just tell me about Alexa. Or, maybe I should leave. I mean, if you —

MIKE.   No. No. Don't leave. I'll tell you.

WYLER.   Really?

MIKE.   Why not? My painting is going slowly. You're cute. You think I'm cute.

WYLER.   I'm not —

MIKE.   Enough tar?

WYLER.   Thank you.

MIKE.   OK, Alexa Vere de Vere.

WYLER.   Where'd her name come from?

MIKE.   We'll get to that later. Before Alexa it was Brenda.

WYLER.   Brenda?

MIKE.   Brenda Gelb. *(Alexa appears as Brenda. A younger girl with long blonde hair and a rough edge or ten. She is in the Eighties.)*

ALEXA.   Brenda Gelb and Mike Stabinsky. WE are soul mates, got it?

MIKE.   I had graduated from Philadelphia College of Art and had gone back home to West Reading, Pennsylvania to earn money for —

ALEXA.   New York City.

MIKE.   And had taken a job working tables in some Amish all you can eat nightmare and. And also working there was a waitress.

ALEXA.   Mike, we gotta get to New York City. We can save enough money if we really scrape, till September and we can get a big loft in Soho and you can paint and I can —

MIKE.   She was just out of high school and she had dreams.

ALEXA.   — be a writer.

WYLER.   To be what?

MIKE.   A writer.

ALEXA.   I can be really great.

WYLER.   *(Laughing.)* Of course. A writer.

ALEXA.   I mean my insights are so uncanny and my vocabulary is just so whatever it's so huge.

MIKE.   So we scrounged and saved and got ourselves to New York.

ALEXA.   Us. Living in New York. Total everything of it all!

MIKE.   It was a great time. We found a hole in the wall space and just, you know homesteaded. I painted. Brenda wrote. We worked graveyard shift at a diner. It was — it was OK, you know?

ALEXA.   Mike, we gotta get some money quick.

MIKE.   But nothing good lasts long.

ALEXA.   I just heard that our beloved day job is going belly up.

WYLER.   What happened?

ALEXA.   They're turning our greasy spoon into a trendy restaurant with models as waiters.

MIKE.   Everything that was good ran away.

ALEXA.   We need something fast or it's back to West Reading.

MIKE.   And we all needed something fast to replace it.

ALEXA.   Art. And fame.

MIKE.   And we all found it. Art and fame.

ALEXA.   Art is exploding, Mike.

WYLER.   Art.

ALEXA.   You can't see your way through the East Village without stepping over a million galleries.

WYLER.   And fame.

ALEXA.   Art art, everywhere you look.

WYLER.   Of course.

ALEXA. And people are buying. And you're better than any-body else out there. How soon can you get a show together? We could make some money here. *(Mike turns to her. They are in the scene together. They are in the Eighties. Wyler watches.)*
MIKE. Brenda —
ALEXA. Mike, you're so good. Look, I know this guy who works down at the copy center and he's semi-dating this guy with a column and he says that when you get a show together, I told him about your work, he is way way intrigued, and he said that his demi-boyfriend would definitely be there. And write it up!
MIKE. I can't get a show together by —
ALEXA. Don't you get it? If you do it, someone will write about it. And if somebody writes about it, somebody else will read about it. And if somebody else reads about it they figured if somebody wrote about it, it must be good and then they buy it! How many paintings do you have done?
MIKE. Seven. Really only one, but the last six I could rush and —
ALEXA. Why do you take so long? What about this one?
MIKE. That's only a color study.
ALEXA. They don't need to know that.
MIKE. Brenda!
ALEXA. It's a seller's market. And seller's markets don't last forever.
MIKE. Art is eternal.
ALEXA. Eternal isn't as long as it used to be.
MIKE. No gallery —
ALEXA. What gallery? We take all the furniture in this loft, right? We move it to one end? Put a drop cloth over it. We have a gallery. Some rancid cheese, some three dollar wine, we've been to enough of these openings, I mean what's the over-head?
MIKE. What would we call it?
ALEXA. I don't know. Something big and foreign and grand and — can you have this done in a month?
MIKE. I mean if I rushed it could — sure, look finished and —

ALEXA.   Foreign with a hyphen. The gallery should have a foreign name with a hyphen.

MIKE.   I've also got some photographs from this class I took in —

ALEXA.   Leibshen-Amore galleries.

MIKE.   Art school, that I could —

ALEXA.   Avanti-L'chat galleries.

MIKE.   Now Brenda we just do this once, for the money then we —

ALEXA.   Fjord-Chang galleries.

MIKE.   Quit it. This is a take the money and run —

ALEXA.   Pesto-Frauline galleries.

MIKE.   Brenda, just name the damn thing, we can sit her coming up with foreign hyphens till we're blue in the face.

ALEXA.   Bluen-DiFace galleries. *(Mike turns to Wyler. Alexa is gone. We are back in the present.)*

MIKE.   And the Bluen-DiFace galleries was born. A quick coat of paint, all the furniture at one end, and I raced like a whirling dervish and managed to whip up six very attractive but entirely pointless paintings. Framed them. And we had the most unique way of pricing things. We'd just shout out a price. And whatever price was so absurd that we had to laugh, that's the price we'd put on it.

WYLER.   What about Alexa Vere de Vere? When did Brenda become Alexa Vere de Vere?

MIKE.   Right. Alexa. OK. Well. Xeroxed off about a hundred invitations and we made lists and we called and we — she — came up with a lot of resistance. *(At one end of the loft, Brenda is on the phone trying to get some attention. Mike walks over and sits near her and watches. We are back in the Eighties.)*

ALEXA.   Hi, this is Brenda Gelb of the Bluen-DiFace galleries and we have an opening and stuff coming up and — it's on — and I know you're busy I can imagine but — maybe on your way to the whatever biennial you could stop by and — oh — there's gonna be wine and — sure I understand. *(Mike looks to Wyler.)*

MIKE.   It was —

WYLER.   Not happening.

MIKE.   Not happening. *(He's back with Brenda.)*

ALEXA.   This is not happening.

MIKE.   Well — I hope you don't mind me — Maybe you sound a little too much like a girl from West Reading, Pennsylvania.

ALEXA.   That would be maybe because ... I am? Just thinking off the cuff.

MIKE.   Well maybe if you sounded like — I don't know —

ALEXA.   Say it.

MIKE.   Like — OK, remember that women at that gallery, the woman who ran the opening of the space on East Ninth? Like her.

ALEXA.   Affected?

MIKE.   Well —

ALEXA.   Snooty?

MIKE.   Flawless.

ALEXA.   Like Alexis on *Dynasty.*

MIKE.   Joan Collins is a little —

ALEXA.   Hello this is Alexis DiFace from the Bluen-DiFace Gallery.

MIKE.   — repulsive. No, your name shouldn't be in the gallery. And Alexis is too — on the money.

ALEXA.   Alexxxxxxa?

MIKE.   Alexa from the Bluen-DiFace gallery.

ALEXA.   Alexa from the Bluen-DiFace gallery.

MIKE.   We'll see. A familiar sounding last name. But not a real name that people can trace.

ALEXA.   Alexa Van Cleef. And Arpels.

MIKE.   Traceable. Possibly.

ALEXA.   And I gotta get flawless. How do I get flawless? *(The lights go out. Only Mike in a spotlight.)*

MIKE.   That weekend we did nothing but rent videos and Brenda learned about flawless. *(Lights out on Mike. Lights up full on Brenda. The blue light of a television is before her. She is talking along with a video tape of Rosalind Russell in* Auntie Mame.*)*

ALEXA.   Help will be here 'ere long, darlings! Mamie Dennis!! *Voila!* Now where is that divine bootlegger, he promises to bring more gin — Aww Raymond *mon chou,* I cannot wait for you to — Eveline, you have not returned my last two phone calls — hello darling be with you in a minute, Gregor, I'm ever so glad you are here! Ha ha oooh. Oh you must hear his new symphony, the pastoral. It has motorcycle motors and live goats on the stage it's debilitating, positively debilitating. Terry!! Morris!! Now where in heaven's name!! *(The blue light goes out quickly. The lights come up on Mike, still trying to come up with a name.)*

MIKE.   Alexa Van Trapp? No. *(The light abruptly goes out on Mike as the blue television light flashes on Brenda. She is standing up and acting out the video tape of Sally Bowles in* Cabaret.*)*

ALEXA.   Frauline Shneider *Nix sum hou* — have you a cigarette? I'm desperate. *(Cigarette is lit.)* Divine decadence. Sally Bowles, here. Come on in Brian, darling. It's the most marvelous boarding house. Wonderful boarders. Nobody has any money, who does these days? To be honest, I'm never around. I tear about all day and then am up all hours at the cabaret. *(A tango is heard.)* I'm not the type with wisdom, Brian darling. I have instincts. *(She dances.)* I have ancient instincts and I have this uncanny, possibly spiritual, thatish feeling about you. That you're going to be my roommate. My roommate. OK? OK? *(She offers a toast.)* Prairie oysters! *(Mike steps into the blue light and ejects the tape.)*

MIKE.   Alexa Vanderbilt?

ALEXA.   I like the V to go with the X. But no van.

MIKE.   God. Beggers can be choosers. *(He puts another video in.)*

ALEXA.   Look. I have to say the name, let me pick it.

MIKE.   You can. Just talk.

ALEXA.   They won't believe me.

MIKE.   They'll believe you because they'll want to believe you. *(He is dialing a number.)*

ALEXA.   But —

MIKE.   After a day full of fucking bores who wouldn't want a call from Alexa Vere de Vere? *(He hands her the receiver.)*

ALEXA.   I can't — *(She takes the receiver and puts it to her ear.)*

MIKE.   Shhhhhhhh. Leo.

ALEXA.   Hello, Alexa Vere de Vere from Bluen-DiFace galleries for Leo. Leo, Alexa Vere de Vere, *Voila!* I never see you anymore. I tear about all day and then am up all hours at the caba — *(A squeeze on the arm from Mike.)* Gallery. I think I saw you last at Tiffany's. I'm CRAZY for Tiffany's. Nothing too awful can happen to you there. Now Darling, the most wonderful gallery. Wonderful artists. Nobody has any money, who does these days. New artist — Michael Stabinski. His work — debilitating, positively devasting. It's Monday the third, I know you'll want to be there. I'll messenger over the invite and — Terry, Morris! What part of the ship were you on? Darling, I must tear. But I have this uncanny, possibly spiritual thatish feeling about you and this artist. See you then? How utterly, utterly cunning. *(She hangs up. She can't believe it.)* He says he'll come.

MIKE. Where did utterly, utterly cunning come from?

ALEXA. I made that one up. *(Alexa is gone. A flash, Mike is back with Wyler..)*

MIKE. Brenda took to Alexa Vere de Vere like a flame to oil. And soon Alexa wasn't just a name we made up it was a game we played. Every chance we had we'd see who could out Alexa the other. She's say, "Are you going to the drug store?" I'd say, "I'm about to pop off to the chemists."

WYLER. Out of control.

MIKE. She was. Completely.

WYLER. Not just her. You. You were out of control.

MIKE. Yeah. I guess I was. But that was the great thing about New York in the eighties. Out of control didn't stick out at all.

WYLER. So. Alexa. What happened next?

MIKE. We laughed a lot. And called an obscene amount of receptive people, who really should have known better until —

WYLER. The opening?

MIKE. Yeah. The opening. No. Just before.

WYLER. God, I'll bet you were excited.

MIKE. Yes. No. Mostly terrified.

WYLER. Terrified? *(Mike walks into the bathroom. We see Alexa bending over a sink, a towel over her head. We are back in the Eighties.)*

MIKE. May I have the sink, I want to vomit.

ALEXA. Vomit in the toilet, you know Michael —

MIKE. Mike.

ALEXA.   Michael, you really must do something about your name. It is but so unruly. How is anyone to take an artist seriously when you end your name with a ski?

MIKE.   Kandinsky?

ALEXA.   The exception that proves the rule. Stop vomiting and relax.

MIKE.   You don't get it. You are so wrapped up in the whatever of it all that — these people, the ones coming tonight are all — they're the people I hope to one day impress with my real work. And they're here because we've ... conned them. We've lied to them. Christ, we've lied to ourselves. We have no business doin —

ALEXA.   Oh Michael.

MIKE.   Mike.

ALEXA.   Michael. We have every bit of business doing this. And what the fuck is this impress others crap?

MIKE.   Brenda, no —

ALEXA.   You yourself have told me myriad —

MIKE.   — no, not like —

ALEXA.   — times that the only person an artist is required to impress is himself.

MIKE.   No, Brenda.

ALEXA.   Yes, we've conned others to get here but once they are here, they are on their own.

MIKE.   You're right.

ALEXA.   And as for the conning of ourselves, all I can say is — we both know who we are. And we know what we've done.

MIKE.   You're ... right. I'm sorry, just opening night jitters. *(She removes her towel. Her hair is in the Alexa black page boy cut.)*

ALEXA.   What do you think?

MIKE.   My God, what have you done?

ALEXA.   I just — when I look in the mirror, I don't want to see Brenda. I want to see Alexa. *(She is gone. Mike looks forward. The bathroom is gone.)*

MIKE.   And we were off. The crowd from the beginning was ... amazing. The room soon filled with people, and Brenda was ... on fire. *(Early Eighties dance music is heard.)* She knew everyone by their first name. And everyone seemed so touched that

56

she had remembered them. Never mind she had never met them, it was just nice she remembered. And the people. It was easy for Brenda slash Alexa to say where'd she seen them. She'd seen them in magazines. One after the other. They marched in. As if someone had suddenly made an issue of "W" in 3-D. Warhol walked by and Alexa kissed him on the hand and said, "Andy Warhol, we are you children!" And Warhol said, "Wow." And for those of us looking for signs, and we were, this was a biggie. Of course later we found out that was pretty much Warhol's response to anything. You could say, "Andy your toupee is on fire" and he'd — "wow." But. But I look back on that time and I am envious. I am nostalgic. I am — I'd like to do it one more time But that is dangerous. For when it was all over and it was just the two of us — *(Mike is holding a canvas. He is alone in the now empty loft. Alexa staggers in with a bottle of champagne. She is wearing early Eighties high fashion gear.)*

ALEXA. Michael? Lamb?

MIKE. Mike.

ALEXA. Success. A ringing success. A ... successful success. Have some champagne. Every painting sold. A miracle in the order of fish and loaves.

MIKE. Every painting. Except one.

ALEXA. All right, every painting except one. Your glass is metaphorically half empty, isn't it?

MIKE. Brenda, the one that didn't sell was ... is —

ALEXA. What?

MIKE. The only one that's finished.

ALEXA. Did anyone like it? What did Warhol say?

MIKE. He said, "WOW." What the FUCK does he ever say?

ALEXA. Don't you bark at me. I will not be — I am SO VERY sorry that we've made thousands of dollars this evening selling everything you've ever touched. And that now you are free to create for the next year. And you are, you know? Michael. Lamb. You are free to create for another year and do what you really want to. And when we're broke, we'll just do another mocked up show and we'll — we get to do what we want, is that such a crime?

MIKE. No. Of course not.

ALEXA.   We get to be whatever we want to be in this life. And so we do take advantage of the art world. May I say? So fucking what? A world that values it's creators more dead? A world of "wow"?

MIKE.   Of course.

ALEXA.   We've done it. We've fucked them over and they've said thank you. We've won.

MIKE.   Of course of course.

ALEXA.   Champagne?

MIKE.   Yeah. *(He takes a swig.)*

ALEXA.   And it was fun.

MIKE.   It was fun.

ALEXA.   I love you.

MIKE.   I love you. *(They kiss.)*

ALEXA.   I love you. *(They look at one another. Not quite knowing what to do.)*

MIKE.   I … love you. *(Alexa closes her eyes and moves towards him for a more passionate kiss.)*

ALEXA.   I love you … Lamb. *(Mike pulls away.)*

MIKE.   Uh — Brenda. This is … just silly. No.

ALEXA.   Come on.

MIKE.   No.

ALEXA.   You can be whatever you want to be.

MIKE.   Oh I think even Norman Vincent Peale would throw his hands up on this one.

ALEXA.   Quickly tear my clothing off. Only gently, I want to return this dress to Berdorf's in the morning.

MIKE.   *(With a laugh.)* No.

ALEXA.   You can be —

MIKE.   I can be whatever I want to be and I want to be a homosexual. Now —

ALEXA.   And you feel —

MIKE.   Now I —

ALEXA.   — nothing? NOTHING —

MIKE.   — think we should —

ALEXA.   Towards me after I —

MIKE.   Just cool off here and —

ALEXA.   After all I've —

58

MIKE. Go to, you know, neutral corners and —

ALEXA. Fucking done for you?!

MIKE. Fucking done for me? Where did that —

ALEXA. You know what your problem is —

MIKE. I wasn't aware of having —

ALEXA. You have success issues.

MIKE. What the fuck —

ALEXA. Fucker. Stupid fucker. After all I've done for you. After all I've fucking done for you and this is how you just choose to fucking repay me?!

MIKE. Brenda — *(Alexa throws money at him.)*

ALEXA. I hate you!! What would it have taken to just —

MIKE. Just —

ALEXA. Given me a little something in return?! Here!

MIKE. Hey!

ALEXA. Here's your fucking half of the money. We are over as of this instant! I never I want to see you again. You are dead to me —

MIKE. Brenda —

ALEXA. Brenda and Mike are dead! Someday you'll fucking know what you lost! *(She is gone. Mike casually picks up the money and continues to talk to Wyler. We slowly move into the present.)*

MIKE. And I never saw her again. Ever. About two years later I bumped into someone in a gallery who had been to my opening. And he fell. It seems Brenda (now exclusively Alexa) had told them that I was dead. Suicide. I had hanged myself from a street lamp outside of a brothel. My body was discovered swinging over a pack of prowling scavenger dogs.

WYLER. Jesus.

MIKE. *Suicide* by George Grosz. 1916. Oil on canvas. She'd manage to leave with a couple of my art books. *(Wyler looks at the canvas.)*

WYLER. This yours?

MIKE. Yes.

WYLER. It's good.

MIKE. The one that didn't sell. Thanks.

WYLER. What's it called?

MIKE. As bees in honey drown. *(Wyler laughs.)* What?

WYLER. Alexa says that all the time.

MIKE. Yet another parting gift for her from my game show of an art career. *(Wyler laughs again.)* You're smiling. You look good smiling.

WYLER. Thanks.

MIKE. It makes your eyes squint. Makes your whole face look like a cow jumped over the moon moon. *(A pause. They just stare at one another. They then both smile.)*

WYLER. Well. Again. Thank you. Thanks for the stroll through the Alexa archives and the ... interesting moon image.

MIKE. Anytime.

WYLER. I ... should get going.

MIKE. I have a better idea.

WYLER. Yeah?

MIKE. Take me to dinner. *(Wyler laughs.)*

WYLER. Uh ... I don't know, I —

MIKE. Then just come by sometime when I'm painting and hang out — We'll have a non-date.

WYLER. This isn't what I want.

MIKE. What do you want?

WYLER. To find Alexa. What do you want?

MIKE. I want a place to go and paint. To be left alone for a while. And when I'm done painting, I want to get together with some friends, have a beer and talk about stuff. And we'll commiserate if my painting went poorly. And celebrate if my painting went well. That's what I want. Rolling Rock if possible. But I'll settle for a scary Japanese thing if that's all you have. *(A pause.)* That was a hint in case you were wondering what to bring to the non-date.

WYLER. Uh. Thank you. I'd really like to. But, I have — I just have.

MIKE. Right. *(Offstage we hear Ginny.)*

GINNY. Mr. Morelli.

MIKE. See ya.

GINNY. Mr. Morelli. Please don't cry.

WYLER. Uh. No. But thank you for everything. The tar. All of it. *(Mike goes back to painting. Wyler goes to the door.)*

GINNY. Mr. Morelli.

WYLER. Thanks. I have to go. *(Wyler runs off. Mike looks back. Sees that Evan has left behind his composition book.)*
MIKE. Bye. Hey, you left your — *(The lights fade on Mike as he picks up the composition book and the lights come up on —)*

Scene 5

A photographer's studio.

Two telephones.

First, the studio. A seamless. The same as the beginning of the play. Ginny, a young violinist walks on timidly. Topless, she is covering her breasts with her crossed arms.

GINNY. Mr. Uhm ... Mr. Morelli. Please don't cry. I'm sorry. I just — It's my mom, she's not what you would call, in any meaning of the word, worldly and she — she wouldn't understand me getting my picture taken without my shirt clutching myself with a vacant yet sensual look on my face. And what it has to do with my violin recitals. But if you think it's what I should do to — please stop crying — if you think it's what I should do to get some recognition and — take my picture. I have my shirt off. You can take my picture. See? *(A flash and the lights go down on Ginny. Then, a spotlight in the darkness. We see Alexa putting down the magazine upon seeing Ginny's picture. She picks up the yellow pages and a phone.)*
ALEXA. Hello! Am I speaking to Ginny Cameron. The Violinist. Now darling, I just saw this barely clad photograph and now I've gone and realized. You must play the score to the film of the story of my life. I want something like *Shindler's List* only cheerier! *(With that, at another end of the stage, the lights come up on Wyler. At a newsstand, he is just putting down the magazine with a picture of Ginny. He picks up a phone.)*
WYLER. Hello is this — Ginny? Ginny, you don't know me — but you are going to — wait are you the violinist in the magazine without the shirt? Great. You are going to maybe be get-

ting a phone call from a woman with the unlikely name of Alexa Vere de — Already? Geez. Well has she — are you planning to meet her — *(Lights up on Morris Kaden.)*

KADEN.   Thursday 1:45, the lobby of the Four seasons.

WYLER.   Do not go to that meeting.

KADEN.   Got it.

WYLER.   She is a con artist, ready to rip you off.

KADEN.   Afternoon tea.

WYLER.   What do you think?

KADEN.   You're a sick man. *(Lights up on Illya.)*

ILLYA.   The Four Seasons, Thursday at 1:45?

KADEN.   But not without your style.

ILLYA.   It's devilish.

WYLER.   She's expecting some young violinist for tea. *(Lights up on Bethany.)*

BETHANY.   The Four Seasons. It'll be so horrible. Of course I'll be there.

WYLER.   The violinist won't be there, but who will be there —

KADEN.   The place will be packed.

WYLER.   All of us. *(Lights up on Skunk.)*

SKUNK.   The Four Seasons!.

ILLYA.   Morris Kaden, Illya Mannon.

WYLER.   Thursday, 1:45, the lobby of the Four Seasons. Alexa Vere de Vere will arrive to meet someone new and hot and, sadly, hungry. What she will find will be a lobby filled with the victims of Alexa Vere de Vere.

ILLYA.   Bethany Vance

KADEN.   Martel Kruskov.

BETHANY.   Skunk.

WYLER.   Cold austere revenge. *(An ocean of voices reciting names. And another ocean of voices saying yes. Onstage the next three lines overlap.)*

ILLYA.   That composer with the animation, the actress with the accents, the investor from Milan, the actor with the great hair who can't act, David Bowie, Iman, Morris Kaden of Delta records, Iman, the Duke of Chichester, Skunk, Bethany Vance, the Pet Shop boys, the singer with the six note range.

KADEN.   The singer with the six note range, the poet who

can't rhyme. Evan Wyler, Skunk, Morris Kaden, Illya Mannon, Bethany Vance, David Bowie, Iman, the Duke of Chichester, the Pet Shop boys. Everyone. The composer with the animation, the actress with the accents. Martel Grushkov.

BETHANY.   Martel Grushkov, The Duke of Chicester, The Pet Shop boys. David Bowie and Iman. Skunk, Morris Kaden and Illya Mannon, the composer with the animation, Martel Grushkov, the actor with the really great hair who can't act. Oh and Evan Wyler. The singer with the six note range. And the investor from Milan. *(Silence crashes.)*

Scene 6

Evan's apartment.

In the West Fifties, a four story walk-up tenement. A mess. Wyler walks in. The closet is open. Hanging inside, his suit. On the inside of the door, a mirror. Wyler taps on the answering machine. As the messages play back, an electronic beep. He takes the jacket out and tries it on.

KADEN.   *(Voice on the machine.)* All right Wyler Evan Wyler. We'll be seeing you in one hour. Can't believe we're going through with this. Just about everyone will be there — *(Wyler looks in the mirror. He smiles. Another electronic beep.)*

ILLYA.   *(Voice on the machine.)* Mr. Wyler, I find your sense of revenge openly delicious. Of course we'll be there. I'm so excited I could — what am I saying — I should be heading uptown. It's in forty minutes. *(Wyler looks at himself in profile.)*

GINNY.   *(Voice on the machine.)* Hello, Mr. Wyler. This is Ginny. Ginny Cameron and — oh God — I thinking I just messed things up. *(Wyler is suddenly attentive. He stands straight in front of the mirror.)* See, uhm, Alexa called right? And just — what you said made me so mad and — Well she just wanted to confirm things and I guess she could sense something in my voice, 'cause — well she pushed me and — *(Wyler is panicking. He looks*

63

at the machine. With that the closet door slowly closes. Alexa is stand-
ing behind it. The reflection of Wyler becomes the actual Alexa.) OK,
I kind of blurted out what you were planning and — I hope
this doesn't ruin things for you. *(The machine ends.)*
ALEXA.   One of the all time great entrances and for the life
of me, I don't have a line to top it.
WYLER.   Alexa, how did you —
ALEXA.   Please, twenty dollars and a super and I could get
into heaven. But no. Nothing. No sentence I could hope to
assemble.... No configuration of words could possibly surpass
the fact that I am here and you are there!
WYLER.   You bitch, give me my money back.
ALEXA.   Long gone. Don't have it to give. But then you knew
that. So, why then have you pursued me?
WYLER.   Revenge.
ALEXA.   Please. No really, why? Because you're in love with
me?
WYLER.   Maybe I was.
ALEXA.   You're a poofta, guess again.
WYLER.   I know who you are and how you work and —
ALEXA.   And now that you do have me again what will you
do?
WYLER.   I — I — I don't know.
ALEXA.   *(She casually sits and lights a cigarette.)* As I had sus-
pected. Planned confrontations are always anti-climactic. I'll
smoke and talk to you. You'll learn things, it will be lovely. I
shall hazard a guess. The reason you have pursued me so
doggedly is because you are the first to know —
WYLER.   Know?
ALEXA.   My lamb. My dearest lamb. My only lamb. You know.
You know that I am not a mirage, I am an oasis. You are the
only, the first. To chase. Most feel the sting and snap their hand
from the bee. You — you actually are stung and ... appear to
be homesick for the hypnotic hum of the hive.
WYLER.   You've got it wrong.
ALEXA.   I have it unspeakably right. The reason no one has
ever chased me, is because they've always had their blessed little artistic endeavors to keep them busy. Writing, dancing,

64

painting, even I would speculate, the fiddle. No one would think of putting this much energy and effort into finding me let alone exacting recompense. This is the defining act of someone who — gets it.

WYLER.   I don't get any of —

ALEXA.   Oh no. You get it. You get it good. You know that this. The hum, the buzz, the hype, the flash, the fame. This is the only thing that matters. And you miss it. Who wouldn't? There is something unmistakably glorious about having a velvet cord pulled back. And you know it. And that's why I come with an offer.

WYLER.   I don't want your fucking —

ALEXA.   I know, an offer it seems too generous.

WYLER.   What? Money to go away?

ALEXA.   Better.

WYLER.   Better?

ALEXA.   Join me.

WYLER.   You're fucked up.

ALEXA.   Beloved Lamb, you have the instincts, why deny them? You know that if you live your life as a writer you will be popular for a decidedly finite time. Fast-paced American culture won't stand for it. If you write novels, sixteen years. Plays, six years. Screenplays ... six months. And then suddenly you're ... out of favor. Stay with me and always be popular. Fame without achievement, it is the safest bet I know.

WYLER.   I'm a writer.

ALEXA.   Funny, you're not writing now. And you'll probably never write again. Because you know, as I knew, that there are only two interesting times to be a writer. The moment you start a project, and the moment you end it. All the rest is just drudgery. Me, here, this way, I start a project every week. And it ends that same week. What could be more thrilling?

WYLER.   Right. And what if I have the desire to express myself artistically?

ALEXA.   Suppress it. It is every time you create that you run the risk of proving or chiseling at your reputation. Come with me, live with me, and always live this life. Never, ever be hungry, or thirsty, or doubt yourself. Or wait in line. Or talk to bores. Or —

WYLER. Why?

ALEXA.   Because, I need you. When we were together, we were a team. A machine, if you will. The two of us, we could hit higher grounds. Hollywood but beckons. I mean morality is REALLY on a bell curve there. We could make our fortune. Maybe stop living so hand to mouth. Or start living larger hand to larger mouth. Come. Come with me. We're a perfect match. And.

WYLER. And?

ALEXA. And I love you. I want you. I have from the moment I saw your shirtless picture in that magazine. And I saw a very Welsh name attached to a very Semitic face. I wanted you, and I knew that you — you would want me also. *(They kiss.)*

WYLER. Alexa — *(They kiss again.)*

ALEXA. My Lamb. *(They kiss a third time, more passionately.)*

WYLER. I've missed you — *(He kisses her neck, she unbuttons his shirt.)*

ALEXA. And I — my love, I have missed you so. Not since — since — I haven't felt this horribly alone since my husband Michael died, the — *(Wyler freezes. Then pulls away.)* He — *(Wyler steps back and looks away.)* Christ, you are thorough.

WYLER. Mike is still alive, you didn't kill him.

ALEXA. Alive, you call that living? I haven't heard of him in years, and I read everything.

WYLER. I think you should just … leave. Now.

ALEXA. A minor glitch. A single *faux pas*. Don't let that stand in the way of our —

WYLER. Get out. Now.

ALEXA. Back to revenge? Well you can't have it. You have no power. You're a commodity, bought and sold. You're a —

WYLER. Get!

ALEXA. Suit!

WYLER. Out!

ALEXA. A suit. Bought this year and then out of fashion.

WYLER. Leave me!

ALEXA.   Fine. I'll leave. Simpleton. But in eleven days. In a week. After staring at blank page after blank page, you'll be —

66

what? Wishing. Hoping. Desperately beseeching to be with me. *(She goes to walk out. We hear offstage.)*

KADEN.   Such a party!

WYLER.   Never!

ALEXA.   You're not a writer.

ILLYA.   The event of a lifetime!

ALEXA.   You're not particularly good at listening to people and figuring out what's going in their minds.

KADEN.   In your whole life.

ALEXA.   Or summing up with a grand sweeping statement.

KADEN.   Could you again see such a group.

ALEXA.   And what good is a semicolon? *(We see Illya and Kaden.)*

ILLYA.   Everyone was there!

ALEXA.   Please. Call me. You'll know where to find me. How to reach me. The beginning of every month. In the magazines. In all those fresh, young, desperate faces. Call them. For I will have. You'll soon find…. You need me, Lamb. *(She is gone. Wyler says to the empty room.)*

WYLER.   I don't need you.

KADEN.   Such the A-list group. *(Wyler runs over to the open door and shouts off to Alexa.)*

WYLER.   I … DO … NOT … NEED … YOU!!

Scene 7

The Four Seasons.

Illya and Kaden give us their report.

ILLYA.   You should have been there —

KADEN.   At the four seasons.

ILLYA.   There must have been —

KADEN.   You should have been there.

ILLYA.   — hundreds. It was fantastic.

KADEN.   It was phenomenal.

67

ILLYA. Everywhere you looked, somebody as famous than the next.

KADEN. A large lobby filled with the victims of the Alexa Vere De Vere.

ILLYA. The famous, the known, the hype-worthy,

KADEN. The renowned, the celebrities, the sub-lebrities.

ILLYA. Household names.

KADEN. Photo-ops.

ILLYA. Faces.

KADEN. Names.

ILLYA. And everyone of us knew.

KADEN. Every one of us knew —

ILLYA. — knew.

KADEN and ILLYA. — it meant nothing.

ILLYA. Nothing at all.

KADEN. But we all —

ILLYA. Every one of us.

KADEN. *(A pause and a smile, then —)* Knew how to play it.

ILLYA. The hype.

KADEN. The buzz

ILLYA. The hum.

Scene 8

Mike's loft.

Mike is painting. A knock on the door. He answers it. It is Wyler.

MIKE. Hey, I know you.

WYLER. Yeah right. Uhm, I was just in the neighborhood, so I thought I'd stop by and —

MIKE. Sure. Listen I've just got to finish this before the paint dries.

WYLER. Sure sure. Go ahead.

MIKE. The color won't match if I do it later. *(He goes back to painting.)*

WYLER.   I'm just in the neighborhood, so. I'm like walking around. And. Actually that's not true. I'm in the neighborhood because I wanted to see you.

MIKE.   Oh.

WYLER.   Not that way. It's just. Everybody else seems so ... I don't know, caught up. I'm kind of lost. At sea. Like uhm. I don't know, would I be flotsam of jetsam?

MIKE.   You got me. You're the writer.

WYLER.   Nah. I — I think I gave that up.

MIKE.   Oh. I'm sorry to hear that.

WYLER.   It is just so — incredibly difficult, you know? To try to create something. And to know that there are so many people waiting to criticize or capitalize and all you want to do is make something that will connect with other people so that we all won't feel so profoundly alone. And we are all so profoundly alone. Why does it have to be so hard to try to cure that in some way. It ... is ... so ... difficult.

MIKE.   Yeah.

WYLER.   Yeah?

MIKE.   Yeah.

WYLER.   Yeah.

MIKE.   You know what else is difficult?

WYLER.   What?

MIKE.   Ears.

WYLER.   Ears?

MIKE.   Ears are real difficult. You've got these little pockets of shadow and crevices and folds and light bouncing off and. Ears are difficult.

WYLER.   Yeah. I never really thought of that.

MIKE.   But I'm getting better at them. The more I work at it. *(He looks at Wyler. Wyler looks away.)*

WYLER.   Why do you even bother?

MIKE.   Well. If I get it right. This could be a really tremendous ear. *(He goes back to painting.)*

WYLER.   I'm sorry to barge in like. This is — I should go and —

MIKE.   You left your uhm —

WYLER.   Sorry?

MIKE. When you were here before. You left your composition thing —

WYLER. God, right. *(He picks it up.)* Well. Useless. You could have thrown it out. *(He opens it to a page.)* Garbage. *(He looks at another page.)*

Scene 9

Deus ex machina.

Immediately following, a Muse appears behind Wyler. She speaks as Illya.

A MUSE. *(As Illya.)* I really don't know her. It was like like one weekend and twenty-five grand. *(Wyler rips the page out of the book. He looks at the next page. A Second Muse appears. She speaks as Bethany.)*

A SECOND MUSE. Fucker rips you off and then claims you into a circle of friends. *(Wyler rips another page. The first Muse is now is now Carla.)*

A MUSE. You look resplendent. *(Wyler rips another page. The Second Muse is now a Backup Singer.)*

A SECOND MUSE. He's a Welshman, he is. *(He rips out one page after another with the next several lines. They are things Alexa has said, but the two Muses speak them.)*

A MUSE. If you absolutely had to sleep with one of the Three Stooges, which one would it be?

A SECOND MUSE. *(Coming in on the "Stooges" of the last sentence.)* I believe in cash, in this flighty world it's the only thing left with any impact.

A MUSE. *(Coming in on the "left" of the last line.)* A WELSH-MAN. I shall trust anyway.

A SECOND MUSE. *(On the "trust" of the last line.)* The new becoming old almost before we find newer new.

A MUSE. *(On the "find" of the last line.)* We beat the path to Hollywoodland —

A SECOND MUSE. Hollywood —

A MUSE.   Do we dare?

A SECOND MUSE.   And look at your face light up.

A MUSE.   *(Simultaneously with the next line.)* You will buy hundreds, nay thousands of suits.

A SECOND MUSE.   *(Simultaneously with the last line.)* After work I needed, nay required a hot bath.

A MUSE.   What care I?

A SECOND MUSE.   Gore Vidal says that.

A MUSE.   Calvin Klein fragrances.

A SECOND MUSE.   I say it too.

BOTH MUSES.   You're not the person you were born. Who wonderful is? You're the person you were meant to be. *(He rips the final page out and crumples it up. He then thinks for a moment. He flattens out the paper and reads it again.)* You're not the person you were born. Who wonderful is? You're the person you were meant to be. *(He absently takes out a pen and writes something. Then looks at it. This has his interest. He begins to write something else on the page. The Muses leave. A moment of the two artists creating and then —)*

MIKE.   What you writing?

WYLER.   *(Absently.)* Nothing. *(Mike is gone. Kaden is in his office. His Secretary walks in.)*

SECRETARY.   Mr. Kaden.

WYLER.   Nothing.

SECRETARY.   Mr. Kaden, you have a call on line three —

KADEN.   I'm going into a meeting.

SECRETARY.   Mr. Kaden, on line three —

KADEN.   I'm —

SECRETARY.   On line three. Alexa Vere de Vere.

KADEN.   You're kidding.

WYLER.   *(With the great joy of realization.)* Everything. *(Alexa is on the phone with Kaden.)*

KADEN.   Alexa?

ALEXA.   Morris, darling, he has really overstepped the bounds of libel.

KADEN.   Alexa, to what do I —

ALEXA.   And he uses YOUR NAME — that has got to be illegal!

KADEN.   My name? Who is using my name?

ALEXA.   I was walking down Fifth Avenue, in the mid forties, a light snow was falling, I merely looked for the reflection in a window to tromp up the *l'eoile,* darling, when there in the window — *(Illya is reading a book.)*

ILLYA.   *As Bees in Honey Drown.*

ALEXA.   A book. The author's name was unknown to me.

WYLER.   A novel by Eric Wollenstein.

ALEXA.   Of course I was intrigued. I burst into the store and grasped a copy. And there —

WYLER.   In a V neck pullover sweater and a button down shirt, leaning on a stack of Proust.

SECRETARY.   "About the author:"

ALEXA.   Evan Wyler! *(Kaden laughs.)*

ILLYA.   "Eric Wollenstein's debut novel, *Pig and Pepper* was published under the pseudonym Evan Wyler. He has written short stories, and —"

ALEXA.   I nervously flipped through to the front of the book.

ILLYA.   "This is his second novel."

MIKE.   "He resides in New York City with painter Mike Stabinsky."

ALEXA.   And he's written it all!

ILLYA.   "Chapter one."

SECRETARY.   *(Turns to an unseen friend, and says of the book she is reading.)* He's very good at listening to people and figuring out what's going on in their minds.

ALEXA.   All of our names and — Morris, we must sue. This is —

SECRETARY.   And summing it up with a grand sweeping statement.

ILLYA.   "Evan walked into the Paramount hotel. He was going to meet Alexa Vere de Vere."

ILLYA and SECRETARY.   "Alexa worked for Morris Kaden of Delta records. Morris and Alexa were very big deals." *(Kaden laughs. Alexa is now crying.)*

ALEXA.   Don't laugh, he — he's — *(Alexa is sobbing.)* He's destroying —

MIKE.   "Soon to be a major motion picture." *(Alexa looks up, she is plotting away. Oh, the possibilities! Wyler walks over to Alexa. He sits next to her. A moment. Illya reads from the book.)*

ILLYA.   "Alexa took a sip of tea."

WYLER.   Which tea are you drinking, the orange pekoe or the Sodium Pentathol.

ALEXA.   Repartee! You are brilliant. God. I love writers. They always have the last word, because they know so many. I'm part Indian, I know things. Do you think David Bowie is dark enough to pull off an Indian? I mean a red-dot Indian not a woo-woo Indian. Try the boysenberry, it's a revelation.

WYLER.   Have you ever thought of diagramming these sentences in your head before you speak them?

ALEXA.   See.

ALEXA and ILLYA.   That's what I mean.

ALEXA, ILLYA and SECRETARY.   Who else but a writer —

ALEXA, ILLYA, SECRETARY and KADEN.   — they know so —

ALEXA, ILLYA, SECRETARY, KADEN and MIKE.   — much about life.

ALEXA.   No one pulls the cashmere over the eyes of a writer. *(Alexa looks at Wyler. Wyler looks out. And smiles. Ars Longa. Vida Brevis.)*

END OF PLAY

PROPERTY LIST

Camera (PHOTOGRAPHER)
Glass of white wine (AMBER)
Cigarette (ALEXA)
Ivory cigarette holder (ALEXA)
Silver tea service, with tea (ALEXA)
Judith Leiber purse with contents (ALEXA)
       pills
       makeup
       wad of cash
Plate of pastry (ALEXA)
Credit card (WYLER, WAITER, SECRETARY)
Cash: 2 20-dollar-bills, 1 10-dollar-bill (ALEXA)
Credit card receipt and pen (WAITER)
Shirt (ALEXA)
Slacks (ALEXA)
Tie (RONALD)
Shoes (ALEXA)
Cash in bills (ALEXA)
Tray of colognes (ALEXA)
Suit bag (ALEXA)
Receipt check (RONALD)
Large shopping bag (RONALD)
Composition book (WYLER, MIKE)
Video tapes (MIKE)
Pencil (WYLER)
Salted nuts
Bottles of champagne
Drink (ALEXA)
Piece of paper (ALEXA)
Cocktails (ALEXA, WYLER)
Bag of clothing (WYLER)
Magazines (WYLER, SECRETARY)
Handkerchief (WYLER)
Quarters (coins) (WYLER)
Glass of water (KADEN)
Paper towels (SECRETARY)

Bandages (SECRETARY)
Stack of magazines (ALEXA)
Cup of coffee (MIKE)
Cigarette, lit (ALEXA)
Towel (ALEXA)
Painting canvases (MIKE)
Bottle of champagne (ALEXA)
Magazines with "Hot Violinist" on cover (ALEXA, WYLER)
Pen (WYLER)

NEW PLAYS

★ **CLOSER by Patrick Marber.** Winner of the 1998 Olivier Award for Best Play and the 1999 New York Drama Critics Circle Award for Best Foreign Play. Four lives intertwine over the course of four and a half years in this densely plotted, stinging look at modern love and betrayal. "CLOSER is a sad, savvy, often funny play that casts a steely, unblinking gaze at the world of relationships and lets you come to your own conclusions ... CLOSER does not merely hold your attention; it burrows into you." –*New York Magazine* "A powerful, darkly funny play about the cosmic collision between the sun of love and the comet of desire." –*Newsweek Magazine* [2M, 2W] ISBN: 0-8222-1722-8

★ **THE MOST FABULOUS STORY EVER TOLD by Paul Rudnick.** A stage manager, headset and prompt book at hand, brings the house lights to half, then dark, and cues the creation of the world. Throughout the play, she's in control of everything. In other words, she's either God, or she thinks she is. "Line by line, Mr. Rudnick may be the funniest writer for the stage in the United States today ... One-liners, epigrams, withering put-downs and flashing repartee: These are the candles that Mr. Rudnick lights instead of cursing the darkness ... a testament to the virtues of laughing ... and in laughter, there is something like the memory of Eden." –*The NY Times* "Funny it is ... consistently, rapaciously, deliriously ... easily the funniest play in town." –*Variety* [4M, 5W] ISBN: 0-8222-1720-1

★ **A DOLL'S HOUSE by Henrik Ibsen, adapted by Frank McGuinness.** Winner of the 1997 Tony Award for Best Revival. "New, raw, gut-twisting and gripping. Easily the hottest drama this season." –*USA Today* "Bold, brilliant and alive." –*The Wall Street Journal* "A thunderclap of an evening that takes your breath away." –*Time Magazine* [4M, 4W, 2 boys] ISBN: 0-8222-1636-1

★ **THE HERBAL BED by Peter Whelan.** The play is based on actual events which occurred in Stratford-upon-Avon in the summer of 1613, when William Shakespeare's elder daughter was publicly accused of having a sexual liaison with a married neighbor and family friend. "In his probing new play, THE HERBAL BED ... Peter Whelan muses about a sidelong event in the life of Shakespeare's family and creates a finely textured tapestry of love and lies in the early 17th-century Stratford." –*The NY Times* "It is a first rate drama with interesting moral issues of truth and expediency." –*The NY Post* [5M, 3W] ISBN: 0-8222-1675-2

★ **SNAKEBIT by David Marshall Grant.** A study of modern friendship when put to the test. "... a rather smart and absorbing evening of water-cooler theater, the intimate sort of Off-Broadway experience that has you picking apart the recognizable characters long after the curtain calls." – *The NY Times* "Off-Broadway keeps on presenting us with compelling reasons for going to the theater. The latest is SNAKEBIT, David Marshall Grant's smart new comic drama about being thirtysomething and losing one's way in life." –*The NY Daily News* [3M, 1W] ISBN: 0-8222-1724-4

★ **A QUESTION OF MERCY by David Rabe.** The Obie Award-winning playwright probes the sensitive and controversial issue of doctor-assisted suicide in the age of AIDS in this poignant drama. "There are many devastating ironies in Mr. Rabe's beautifully considered, piercingly clear-eyed work ..." –*The NY Times* "With unsettling candor and disturbing insight, the play arouses pity and understanding of a troubling subject ... Rabe's provocative tale is an affirmation of dignity that rings clear and true." –*Variety* [6M, 1W] ISBN: 0-8222-1643-4

★ **DIMLY PERCEIVED THREATS TO THE SYSTEM by Jon Klein.** Reality and fantasy overlap with hilarious results as this unforgettable family attempts to survive the nineties. "Here's a play whose point about fractured families goes to the heart, mind – and ears." –*The Washington Post* "... an end-of-the millennium comedy about a family on the verge of a nervous breakdown ... Trenchant and hilarious ..." –*The Baltimore Sun* [2M, 4W] ISBN: 0-8222-1677-9

DRAMATISTS PLAY SERVICE, INC.
440 Park Avenue South, New York, NY 10016 212-683-8960 Fax 212-213-1539
postmaster@dramatists.com www.dramatists.com

NEW PLAYS

★ AS BEES IN HONEY DROWN by Douglas Carter Beane. Winner of the John Gassner Playwriting Award. A hot young novelist finds the subject of his new screenplay in a New York socialite who leads him into the world of *Auntie Mame* and *Breakfast at Tiffany's*, before she takes him for a ride. "A delicious soufflé of a satire ... [an] extremely entertaining fable for an age that always chooses image over substance." *–The NY Times* "... A witty assessment of one of the most active and relentless industries in a consumer society ... the creation of 'hot' young things, which the media have learned to mass produce with efficiency and zeal." *–The NY Daily News* [3M, 3W, flexible casting] ISBN: 0-8222-1651-5

★ STUPID KIDS by John C. Russell. In rapid, highly stylized scenes, the story follows four high-school students as they make their way from first through eighth period and beyond, struggling with the fears, frustrations, and longings peculiar to youth. "In STUPID KIDS ... playwright John C. Russell gets the opera of adolescence to a T ... The stylized teenspeak of STUPID KIDS ... suggests that Mr. Russell may have hidden a tape recorder under a desk in study hall somewhere and then scoured the tapes for good quotations ... it is the kids' insular, ceaselessly churning world, a pre-adult world of Doritos and libidos, that the playwright seeks to lay bare." *–The NY Times* "STUPID KIDS [is] a sharp-edged ... whoosh of teen angst and conformity anguish. It is also very funny." *–NY Newsday* [2M, 2W] ISBN: 0-8222-1698-1

★ COLLECTED STORIES by Donald Margulies. From Obie Award-winner Donald Margulies comes a provocative analysis of a student-teacher relationship that turns sour when the protégé becomes a rival. "With his fine ear for detail, Margulies creates an authentic, insular world, and he gives equal weight to the opposing viewpoints of two formidable characters." *–The LA Times* "This is probably Margulies' best play to date ..." *–The NY Post* "... always fluid and lively, the play is thick with ideas, like a stock-pot of good stew." *–The Village Voice* [2W] ISBN: 0-8222-1640-X

★ FREEDOMLAND by Amy Freed. An overdue showdown between a son and his father sets off fireworks that illuminate the neurosis, rage and anxiety of one family – and of America at the turn of the millennium. "FREEDOMLAND's more obvious links are to *Buried Child* and *Bosoms and Neglect*. Freed, like Guare, is an inspired wordsmith with a gift for surreal touches in situations grounded in familiar and real territory." *–Curtain Up* [3M, 4W] ISBN: 0-8222-1719-8

★ STOP KISS by Diana Son. A poignant and funny play about the ways, both sudden and slow, that lives can change irrevocably. "There's so much that is vital and exciting about STOP KISS ... you want to embrace this young author and cheer her onto other works ... the writing on display here is funny and credible ... you also will be charmed by its heartfelt characters and up-to-the-minute humor." *–The NY Daily News* "... irresistibly exciting ... a sweet, sad, and enchantingly sincere play." *–The NY Times* [3M, 3W] ISBN: 0-8222-1731-7

★ THREE DAYS OF RAIN by Richard Greenberg. The sins of fathers and mothers make for a bittersweet elegy in this poignant and revealing drama. "... a work so perfectly judged it heralds the arrival of a major playwright ... Greenberg is extraordinary." *–The NY Daily News* "Greenberg's play is filled with graceful passages that are by turns melancholy, harrowing, and often, quite funny." *–Variety* [2M, 1W] ISBN: 0-8222-1676-0

★ THE WEIR by Conor McPherson. In a bar in rural Ireland, the local men swap spooky stories in an attempt to impress a young woman from Dublin who recently moved into a nearby "haunted" house. However, the tables are soon turned when she spins a yarn of her own. "You shed all sense of time at this beautiful and devious new play." *–The NY Times* "Sheer theatrical magic. I have rarely been so convinced that I have just seen a modern classic. Tremendous." *–The London Daily Telegraph* [4M, 1W] ISBN: 0-8222-1706-6

DRAMATISTS PLAY SERVICE, INC.
440 Park Avenue South, New York, NY 10016 212-683-8960 Fax 212-213-1539
postmaster@dramatists.com www.dramatists.com